The

Genius

of

Instinct

The

Genius

of

Instinct

Reclaim Mother Nature's Tools for Enhancing
Your Health, Happiness, Family, and Work

Dr. Hendrie Weisinger

Vice President, Publisher: Tim Moore
Associate Publisher and Director of Marketing: Amy Neidlinger
Acquisitions Editor: Jennifer Simon
Editorial Assistant: Pamela Boland
Development Editor: Russ Hall
Operations Manager: Gina Kanouse
Digital Marketing Manager: Julie Phifer
Publicity Manager: Laura Czaja
Assistant Marketing Manager: Megan Colvin
Cover Designer: Sandra Schroeder
Managing Editor: Kristy Hart
Project Editor: Jovana San Nicolas-Shirley
Copy Editor: Geneil Breeze
Proofreader: San Dee Phillips
Indexer: Joy Dean Lee
Compositor: Jake McFarland
Manufacturing Buyer: Dan Uhrig

This book is sold with the understanding that neither the author nor the publisher is engaged in rendering legal, accounting, or other professional services or advice by publishing this book. Each individual situation is unique. Thus, if legal or financial advice or other expert assistance is required in a specific situation, the services of a competent professional should be sought to ensure that the situation has been evaluated carefully and appropriately. The author and the publisher disclaim any liability, loss, or risk resulting directly or indirectly, from the use or application of any of the contents of this book.

FT Press offers excellent discounts on this book when ordered in quantity for bulk purchases or special sales. For more information, please contact U.S. Corporate and Government Sales, 1-800-382-3419, corpsales@pearsontechgroup.com. For sales outside the U.S., please contact International Sales at international@pearson.com.

Company and product names mentioned herein are the trademarks or registered trademarks of their respective owners.

Printed in the United States of America

First Printing March 2009

ISBN-10: 0-13-235702-X
ISBN-13: 978-0-13-235702-9

Pearson Education LTD.
Pearson Education Australia PTY, Limited.
Pearson Education Singapore, Pte. Ltd.
Pearson Education North Asia, Ltd.
Pearson Education Canada, Ltd.
Pearson Educacio[ac]n de Mexico, S.A. de C.V.
Pearson Education—Japan
Pearson Education Malaysia, Pte. Ltd.

Library of Congress Cataloging-in-Publication Data

Weisinger, Hendrie.

  The genius of instinct : reclaim Mother Nature's tools for enhancing your health, happiness, family, and work / Hendrie Weisinger.

    p. cm.

  ISBN-13: 978-0-13-235702-9 (hardback : alk. paper)

  ISBN-10: 0-13-235702-X (hardback : alk. paper) 1. Instinct. 2. Success. 3. Self-help techniques. I. Title.

  BF685.W45 2009

  650.1—dc22

                              2008026767

To Shovi and Mazel, two Hall of Fame
dogs whose play and love inspired this book.
Their barks will live forever.

Contents

Acknowledgments

Acknowledgments are always my favorite part of my books because I get to thank the people who helped me.

First up is Katie Wiesel. After reading a few pages, Katie took the initiative, and her shelter-seeking instincts found my book a home. Without Katie, there would be no book, and the best part is that she did not take 15 percent!

I was lucky to have Jennifer Simon as my editor. First, her editorial insights significantly shaped the book's landscape, making it broader and more practical. Second, she thought of a great title that captured the book's essence.

While it is true that every ship must sail, I am grateful to publisher Tim Moore for letting my ship sail at its own speed and to be a captain who listens and responds to his crew and prevents the author from being thrown overboard.

Russ Hall helped make the manuscript much more accessible, and his suggestions were very helpful.

Thanks to all the production staff who made the book read and look good!

I wish I personally knew the many scholars whose work inspired my thoughts. Reading their writings was a journey of education and insight, and a curiosity motivator. These evolutionary experts include Matt Ridley, Shelly Taylor, Robert Trivers, Carroll Izard, Nigel Nicholson, Michael McCullough, Leda Cosmides, John Tooby, Alan Miller, Satoshi Kanazawa, David Buss, David Berlyne, and William James. I hope all these people are pleased with the ways I've shown how their work can help people thrive.

The Aresty Institute of Executive Education at the Wharton Business School, UCLA Anderson Graduate School of Management, and The Institute for Management Studies have continued to be supportive of my work, and I am honored to be associated with each.

Dr. Ken Cinnamon proved to be a great sounding board and kept me on the creative path. He continually reminded me that I had something special. Dr. Mel Kinder helped me develop key themes and the ways to present them to benefit my readers. Steve Gold allowed me to "test" the content, Terry Schmidt provided positive expectations, and Simon helped me purify my thoughts. Dr. Ron Podell applied his craft, so naturally, I was cool, calm, and collected throughout this project. Dr. Podell's thoughts on emotional survival were also illuminating and educational. All these people, over the last few decades, have used their care-giving instincts with me in different ways and have helped me secure my niche.

My mother, Thelma, who is still well connected to her maternal instincts and is even better connected to her "grand-maternal instincts," gets the first copy of this book.

Instinctually, of course, I acknowledge my family—Lorie, Bri, and Danny, who continue to be the reservoir for the joys in my life.

About the Author

Dr. Hendrie Weisinger is trained in clinical, counseling, and organizational psychology. His work is known internationally. A *New York Times* bestselling author, he is a leading authority on the application of emotional intelligence, an expert in anger management, and the originator of the highly regarded techniques of criticism training. He has consulted to and conducts workshops for numerous Fortune 500 Companies, including IBM, AT&T, Intel, Motorola, Merrill Lynch, State Farm, The Hartford, Morgan Stanley, Wachovia Securities, Wells Fargo, Medtronic, Chase Manhattan, Nabisco, General Dynamics, Bank of America, Hughes Aircraft, TRW, Control Data, Nintendo, Merck, Avon, Hyatt, Sheraton, and Estée Lauder, to name just a few.

Dr. Weisinger's expertise has also been sought out by government agencies, including the U.S. Justice Department, IRS, EPA, Secret Service, National Security Agency, FBI, and others. In addition, Dr. Weisinger has repeatedly addressed numerous professional and educational organizations, such as the Young Presidents Organization.

Dr. Weisinger is the author of several successful books. His first, *Nobody's Perfect*, reached *The New York Times* Bestseller List. *Dr. Weisinger's Anger Workout Book*, published in 1985, is now in its 27th printing. *Anger at Work*, a 1995 release, was hailed by the *Journal of the Library of Congress* as a book that "managers at all levels will find useful. Highly recommended." His book *Emotional Intelligence at Work* is considered to be the best book on the application of emotional intelligence, and *The Emotionally Intelligent Financial Advisor* is the first book on emotional intelligence customized to a specific industry. His book *The Power of Positive Criticism* has already been translated into ten languages.

Dr. Weisinger has made more than 500 appearances on major television news and information programs, including *The Today Show* (several times, including five consecutive days for its show on anger), *Oprah*, and *Good Morning America*, and on other television and radio programs on CNN, CNBC, and NPR.

His work has been featured in numerous newspapers and national magazines, including *The New York Times* Sunday Business Section, *USA Today*, and *BusinessWeek*. His article for *The Wall Street Journal*, "So You're Afraid to Criticize Your Boss," was selected by Dow Jones as one of the 60 best articles published, and his article for *TV Guide*, "Tutored by Television," is an example of how parents can help their children develop their emotional intelligence.

Dr. Weisinger has taught, and currently teaches, in many leading executive education and executive MBA programs, including Wharton, UCLA, NYU, MIT, Cornell, and Wake Forest.

You may contact Dr. Weisinger at Hweisinger@msn.com.

Introduction

Back to Basics

I bet you've heard and maybe even believe the familiar saying that animals are "ruled by instinct" and man is "ruled by reason," and that is why we are more "evolved" than other animals. Well, forget it!

I've discovered exactly the *opposite* to be true, and this discovery and accompanying revelations are the basis for the three powerful themes presented in this book. They are powerful because each one significantly impacts the daily quality of your life.

The first theme is that human behavior is more flexibly intelligent than that of other animals because *we have—not fewer—but more instinctual tools*. The message for you here is that *you already have* what it takes to enhance all aspects of your life. In fact, you are hard-wired to be successful!

The second theme is that man has "lost contact" with his instincts, and as a result, more often than not, we act *counterinstinctually*. People get themselves in trouble when they are *instinctually disconnected*. I'm sure you've said many times, "I should have listened to my instincts."

The third and most powerful theme is that you can enhance all aspects of your life—your marriage, family, parenting, work, and business—by *reconnecting with your instincts and strategically using the instinctual tools* that Mother Nature evolved in you.

Indeed, when you reflect on the content to be presented and apply it to your observations of the world, you will see that the most broadly successful individuals and organizations are those that utilize the genius of their instincts.

Each of these themes is progressively developed and illustrated. A brief introduction to each theme gets you started in taking advantage of the genius of *your* instincts.

You're Hardwired for Success

You're hardwired for success—that's a bold statement but one that is amply supported by the sciences, specifically evolutionary psychology, which is rapidly becoming the most important of the human sciences and is the theoretical foundation for this book.

Let me be clear that this is *not* a book about evolutionary psychology—many of those books have been written. Rather, it is about how you can use evolutionary concepts to enhance all realms of your life. Indeed, in my quest to study, observe, understand, explain, and predict human behavior, I've found numerous concepts and findings to draw on in evolutionary psychology that present a provocative and new scientific perspective for understanding human behavior, one that contradicts many of the traditional schools of psychological thought.

What makes evolutionary psychology—nicknamed *the new science of the mind*—so revolutionary is that it applies the process of *natural selection* to the development of the brain/mind/intelligence.

Natural selection is simple but decisive. Creatures within a species that possess an advantageous trait that helps them survive live to reproduce, and this trait gets passed down. Over successive generations, species' abilities specialize to succeed in their specific habitat. For example, nocturnal hunters possess acute hearing and specialized night vision. Predators develop speed, power, and weaponry: sharp teeth, beaks, and claws. Some creatures become highly refined specialists adapted to a localized niche, such as the giant panda, which can survive only in bamboo groves. Others become generalists, such as scavenging rodents that can prosper under many conditions.

Instead of viewing the mind as a blank slate at birth that is developed by a bombardment of information, or that our mind consists of a few general learning mechanisms that let us acquire a nearly infinite range of response to different environmental conditions, evolutionary psychology via natural selection enlightens us by revealing that the mind is actually an *evolved collection of mechanisms—instincts—* designed to solve problems of survival.

Generation after generation, for ten million years, natural selection slowly sculpted, or hardwired, into the human brain and the brains of other creatures specific strategies vital to survival and reproduction. The skills that proved successful over time endured because they enabled early man—and modern humankind today—to solve *adaptive problems*, whether it was finding a good cave to live in or a good company to work for, organizing a hunting party or getting your team to work together, teaching the young to survive or developing leaders. Those who were successful at solving these adaptive problems solidified their "ecological niche," their place in the world.

You have an enormous number of instincts that help you survive. This book, though, is not about surviving; it is about thriving. I have chosen to focus on six broad instincts. Becoming aware of them, and using them, will teach you to use your natural genius to truly thrive and prosper.

In subsequent chapters, you explore each of these instinctual tools and the numerous ways in which they can help you enhance your life. As you read through the book, you learn that they are all interrelated—each one supports the next:

- Shelter seeking—Helps you get into an empowering environment
- Care soliciting—Helps you protect your vulnerabilities
- Care giving—Helps you develop others
- Beauty—Helps you get others to desire you
- Cooperation—Helps you stimulate and develop fair and productive relationships
- Curiosity—Helps you stay ahead of the pack

Mother Nature boldly tells us that these six instinctual processes are your evolved tools for continually enhancing your health, happiness, creativity, family, and community. And the fact is, they have worked for hundreds of thousands of years—otherwise, according to natural selection, you would not have this natural genius today.

What, exactly, do we mean by *instinct*? It's a debated concept in the sciences. As you would expect, numerous "experts" have their own definitions for instinct, but most researchers agree on four *instinctual properties* mandatory for a behavior to qualify as a true instinct:

- It is structured for solving a specific survival (adaptive) problem.
- It develops in all normal human beings.
- It develops without any conscious effort and in the absence of any formal teaching.
- It is applied without conscious awareness of its underlying logic.

I will use the concept of instinct in the broader concept of human nature. *Human nature* refers to the daily behaviors, feelings, thoughts, and emotions you have that are instinctually rooted. Thus, the genius of your instincts is the best of human nature.

Instinctual Disconnection

My consulting and clinical experiences over the past four decades have led me to the conclusion that most people are instinctually disconnected. They have "lost contact" with their instincts, and more often than not, being "ruled by reason" often leads to failure, not success.

Numerous times executives have told me they ignored their instincts and made decisions based instead on spreadsheet data—with disastrous results. Dozens of individuals have told me they chose a course of action even though "It didn't feel right." I've heard count-less students say, "I should have known this was the wrong school for me." Many managers have told me, "I went against my instincts and hired him." Of course, we have all heard a variation on that: "I knew I never should have married her."

I've uncovered many reasons for instinctual disconnection, but what is most shocking to me as a psychologist are the countless expe-riences that show so many people in the working world are *completely clueless* to their detachment from their instincts of success, even when their poor results smack them in the face. It is mind-boggling how many people present themselves in an unkempt, slovenly manner and are then surprised when they don't get the sales rep job that mandates a professional appearance. It is startling to think of the dozens of exec-utives who have derailed promising careers and are stunned to dis-cover that it's because they are abrasive or cold to their staff. I am stunned at the number of people who find their job or a task difficult but never ask others for help or mentoring. This is more than instinc-tual disconnection, it is *instinctual blindness*.

Because we are all unique, we all have different reasons—some more universal than others—why we are instinctually disconnected. Throughout the book, I present some of the common reasons—gath-ered from corporate coaching, consulting, teaching, seminar experi-ences, and clinical practice with individuals and couples—why people in work, family, and marriage environments disconnect from their natural instincts. As we go on this journey together, I implore you to stop reading now and then to think about the concepts, to reflect on the factors that might be causing you to be disconnected from your primal instincts.

Regardless of the reason, instinctual disconnection results in you losing the guidance of your instincts and, therefore, handicaps your chances for success, vibrant health, authenticity, and happiness.

Life Enhancement

From my studies and work experiences during the last ten years, I've come to realize that the evolutionary psychology-shaded concepts have great value when strategically applied to the everyday scenarios we encounter, at home and at work. They help us solve a multitude of problems that often stymie us and help us achieve results that impact our life for the better.

I've learned (and so will you, the reader), many specifics, such as how to use your evolved instinctual tools to resolve marital discord, enhance your marriage, including the sex, and become a more attractive mate. I've also learned how evolutionary psychology concepts can help you leave the relationship and job in which you have felt trapped for years.

I've learned how your instinctual tools can help you have better health, lose weight, and bring the family budget under control. I've learned how parents can use evolutionary psychology concepts to advance their child's creativity, stimulate their interests, transform sibling rivalry into sibling support, and create more family fun. Also, evolutionary psychology can teach you how to help your college-bound son or daughter select the right school, and how to get them to help with family chores.

My corporate consulting and teaching experiences have enabled me to understand and learn how companies and individuals can use evolutionary psychology concepts to attract new clients, manage interdepartmental conflict, give an effective presentation, select the right job, and become a more effective executive. It will become obvious to you as you read that the advice gleaned from evolutionary psychology offers the world real solutions for real problems.

What I find most exciting is that this perspective will help you enlighten yourself to the *revelation of what the natural tools for success are in work and at home—with your family, with your partner.*

My goal, then, is to teach you how *to instinctually reconnect* so that you can apply your instinctual tools in innovative ways that enhance your life in all aspects and thus realize the genius of your instincts.

Part I

Shelter Seek...
So You Can Find Your Home

Enhance your life by using your shelter seeking instincts

1 ————————————

Selecting an Empowering Environment

Your Evolutionary Heritage

Any roost used by female bats must provide a safe and secure environment that protects them from predators and adverse weather conditions, as well as providing a microclimate conducive to the growth of their offspring while in the womb and after they are born. It must also be a space with design features that allow the bats to interact socially.

It's not surprising that you would encounter a nest of bats in an old vacated building or church: The bats are there because of their shelter seeking instincts; they have found an environment that suits their needs and allows them to perpetuate themselves.

Studies show that bats living in buildings enter a state of torpor, or deep sleep, less often than bats living in rocky outcrops or caves. Because they enter torpor less frequently, the bats can be more active on more days, giving them increased time to grow and develop their fetus and give birth earlier than those in rock roosts.

Bats in buildings are also better energy conservers than other bats, such as cave dwellers. By roosting in the warmer microenvironments of buildings, females can reach higher body temperatures during the day, and juveniles can achieve higher body temperatures during the night when females are away foraging. Being inside the building helps juveniles grow more quickly, and young building-roosting bats fledge earlier than rock-roosting bats.

In effect, the bats have put themselves in an environment that protects them against predators, helps them save energy, allows them to give birth earlier, and lets their young to grow faster. Their shelter seeking instincts have allowed them to find an empowering environment, or in their case, the ultimate bat cave.

Getting yourself into an empowering environment is the foundation for enhancing your life, according to Mother Nature.

Your Environment of Evolutionary Adaptedness

Life cannot exist in a vacuum, so for every living creature, there is an environment that it must adapt to if it is to survive, an *Environment of Evolutionary Adaptedness (EEA)*. Different species have different EEAs, but the common denominator of each is that it presents standard challenges that tax the adaptive capacities of its inhabitants, whether that environment is a desert or a polar region.

Environment refers to anything external to the organism that impacts its existence, whether it is an ocean, a tree, or another creature.

Shelter seeking has evolved in humans so that we can, like the bat, get ourselves into environments where the externals we interact with are favorable to our existence and enhance our lives.

To take advantage of the genius of your shelter-seeking instinct, I suggest that you think of your environment as anything external to you that impacts your existence at work and at home. Your boss, colleagues, clients, partner, children, house, and office are all parts of your EEA. To get a little ahead of ourselves, start to ponder whether these surroundings make you feel good.

Despite the fact that animals and humans can adapt to their environment, literally thousands of studies show, independent of the individual, the adverse effects that result when an animal or human is in a "negative environment."

Thus, while every environment offers life a chance, some environments are more conducive to enhancing life than others.

Surviving More Than Thriving

I am not going out on the limb to make the generalization that many, many people—be it in their work environment or their marriage environment—are closer to "surviving" than "thriving."

"How are you doing?" is the question, and, "Hanging in there"; "Taking one day at a time"; "Not bad"; "Okay"; and "Getting by" are the answers from the straw man. Surviving—just enough money to pay the bills, getting through a job that's just a living, or dealing with daily marital stresses—for too many people is as good as it gets.

Why do people stay in environments that prevent them from flourishing, be it a marriage or a job? I've heard all sorts of reasons that aid in people disconnecting from their instinct to seek different shelter, and I am sure you have your own too, especially if you are one of those folks in a nonempowering environment.

Some people blame extenuating circumstances: "I stay married for the kids." Others state a lack of options: "There is no other job for me." Also popular is: "The grass isn't any greener elsewhere." Each pat response shares the perception that all "environments" are the same. While it is certainly true that all environments present problems, we all know people who left their old environment—be it a marriage, job, college, community—and are thriving in their new grounds.

Understanding your evolutionary heritage provides another reason that explains why people tend to be disconnected from their shelter seeking instincts and, thus, remain in anemic settings.

Hardwired to Stay

The biggest barrier to using your shelter seeking instincts is that you are hardwired to be *loss averse*. Back in the days when your ancestors were hunter-gatherers, for survival it was imperative to hold on to things, such as food and water. Losing them would spell disaster, so people who held on to things gave themselves an advantage for survival. In so doing, they became more and more loss averse. In fact, being loss averse would explain greed and hoarding—why people keep and want more than is functional.

Unfortunately, hundreds of thousands of years later, you still have it in you to be loss averse. That means, it is hard for you—all of us, really—to let things go, even if it is a bad relationship or an unfulfilling job. We tend to cling because we are loss averse (not codependent).

I have asked many people how they knew it was time to make a change in their surroundings, be it a marriage or a job. Here's a summary of response:

- "I was unhappy at work. My assignments weren't very interesting. I felt I needed to leave."
- "I gave the school a chance. I kept telling myself next semester would be different. After five semesters, I finally concluded I was in the wrong environment. I needed to transfer and I did."
- "I left my marriage in order to survive."
- "Nothing was happening for me. It had to be better somewhere else."

When I heard and analyzed each of these responses I noted that underlying each was a sense of despair, a feeling of desperation—for example, "I had to leave my marriage to survive."

The lesson here is: *Unless your interaction with the environment is really bad, most likely, you are not going to leave.* (Later, we explore how to make this point work for you.)

Being hardwired to be loss averse, you are more likely to learn how to you use your most basic instinct—self-preservation—and, like an animal, learn how to "adapt" to your environment. Many people do this by lowering their expectations, and many others choose to emotionally insulate themselves from those who surround them. These "self-preservation" strategies help people survive their environment—like an animal—but paradoxically, keep them stuck in an environment that prevents them from thriving.

Humans are not meant to survive like animals; they are meant to thrive. Applying the standards of evolutionary psychology, self-preservation simply by the continuance of physical life (surviving a marriage or a job) is not enough. In human nature, there is something more—a desire for self-development. It is this desire that leads to life enhancement. When someone does not feel that he is in an environment that provides adequate scope for self-expression, he experiences a sense of incompleteness and imperfection, a feeling of quiet desperation. These types of feelings lead people to say, "I feel trapped," with the tag line, "Nothing I can do about it except adapt and survive."

You are not trapped.

Beyond Self-Preservation

A recurring and important concept in understanding your evolutionary heritage is *interaction*. In the context of shelter seeking, it means that you are not pushed around by your environment; you respond to it, you interact with it, and the degree to which you can interact with it effectively is crucial to your success.

One implication of the *interactive principle* is that *instead* of interacting by either *adapting* by changing yourself, you have the capacity to *change it*, to *adjust* the dynamics of your environment so that you can thrive. Indeed, human ingenuity has altered every aspect of our environments to enhance human life—from the invention of agriculture and the domestication of animals, which stabilized the food supply and allowed early man to settle in one area, to science and medicine, which have greatly lengthened the human life span and heightened the quality of life. This active ability allows you to convert a hazardous environment—whether it be a so-so marriage or a boring job—into an empowering environment that helps you grow.

A second implication of the interactive concept, and a *gigantic* difference between humans and other mammals, is that humans can and do consciously expose themselves to stimuli that no creature ever would. I doubt your pet dog or cat would voluntarily sit on a roller coaster, or jump off a cliff for sport. Thus, you not only have the capacity to *leave* a specific environment, you also have the capacity to expose yourself to new and potentially more empowering environments. This instinctual genius allows you to make better choices for the quality of your life, from finding the right mate, to finding the right job. Remember, your ancestors were hunter-gathers. They were on the move, always seeking out an environment that would be more empowering to their clan.

In sum, shelter seeking allows you to move beyond a self-preservation survival mode by helping you either find a more empowering environment or adjust the ones that surround you. In other words, instead of adapting or escaping, Mother Nature would say it is better to seek out or adjust if you want to thrive.

Knowing *when* to seek out and adjust is next on the shelter-seeking instinctual agenda.

2 ———————————————

The Face of Emotions

The evolutionary function of emotions is a chief strategic concept, and its implications and applications surface throughout this book, so some details here will also be of value later. It is particularly important, for instance in the context of shelter seeking, to know when it's best for you to *leave* a particular environment, to know when you are in an environment that is the *right match* for you, and to know how to use that environment so you can leave a job or relationship that has you trapped.

Emotional Functioning

Why do humans have emotions? According to the principles of natural selection, they must give some advantage in helping humans survive. What is it?

Unlike the majority of the scientists who study the brain as the hardwiring apparatus for emotions, those who consider your evolutionary heritage use a different part of the body, a different hardwiring apparatus that helps them explain the primary functions of emotions. This hardwiring apparatus is known as your *face*.

The face is the supreme center for sending and receiving social signals crucial for the development of an individual's interpersonal communication and that individual's cohesiveness with family and society.

There is no doubt that facial expressions of emotions have evolutionary-biological significance as a prelude to their psychological and social significance. Contemporary theorists in the field support the belief that facial expressions evolved primarily from *serviceable associated habits* or *intention movements*—the incomplete or preparatory phases of activities, such as attack, locomotion, defense, and movements associated with respiration and vision.

During the course of evolution, facial expression developed into a system of social communication that conveys information about the internal states (intentions) of the expresser and alerts fellow creatures to certain aspects of the environment. For example, a fearful face signals the perception of danger and the intention of the organism to flee or submit.

The importance of facial expressions and facial movements in social communication among primates has been noted by almost every student of primate behavior and, if you were to review the theory and research on the evolution of facial expressions, you would arrive at similar conclusions that help make the case for why you have emotions, and thus, how to best use them for shelter seeking, or for that matter, how to get out of the proverbial self-destructive relationship, that has been going on for years.

First, the facial neuromuscular mechanisms—the muscles, for example, that are necessary to smile or frown and share other basic expressions—show continuity from the higher primates to man. Logically, if human facial expressions are more complex and show greater range and number than the facial displays of lower primates, and yet encompass the facial expressions of lower primates, then evolutionary selection must have played an important role in the differentiation of the emotions and the facial expressions that communicate them.

This being the case, then, different emotions should have different adaptive functions. Studies show this to be true, for example, by showing strong evidence for the existence of genetically determined universal behavior patterns that represent several fundamental emotions. Importantly, findings show that significant aspects of emotion communication are based on genetically programmed and species-common behavior patterns—the facial expressions of the fundamental emotions.

All human social bonds or interpersonal relationships are based on emotions, and the emotions are communicated primarily by means of facial expressions.

Thus, evolutionary sciences tell us that the function of an emotion is to *communicate information*. Strategic evolutionary psychology would instruct you to leverage this function by recognizing and responding to the *message* of your emotion.

When is it time to shelter seek? When your emotions tell you to.

Functional Distress

How do your emotions tell you that your environment is serving you well, or that you are satisfied? If you feel engaged, productive, interested, and do not have the urge to seek out a new environment nor the inclination to escape your present one, then your feelings are telling you that you're in a good place.

On the other hand, if you feel sad, downhearted, and discouraged at work, or lonely, isolated, and miserable in your marriage, then your feelings are telling you that it might be time to *seek out new shelter* or *adjust*.

Distress is a fundamental emotion that has an important evolutionary function—it communicates to the self and others that *all is not well*, and, as such, sparks your urge to either change your habitat or leave it. People experience the urge to seek new shelter when they feel distress, whether caused by a dead-end job or a loveless marriage; distress is the motivator to find a new environment. It might appear that the urge is instigated by the incentive of something better, but, in fact, the seeking instincts are more often aroused by dissatisfaction with the status quo.

Distress Awareness

To put a face on the emotion, visualize: Eyebrows arched upward and inward, sometimes forming a pie-shaped arch in the lower middle forehead. The inner corners of the upper eyelids are drawn up, and the lower eyelid is pushed upward. The corners of the mouth are drawn downward and the chin muscle is pushed upward and raises the center of the lower lip. To really see it, sit in front of a mirror and put on a "distressed face."

Think of your dominant Environments of Evolutionary Adaptedness—your work environment and relationships. What are the pervasive emotional moods that characterize them, and what do they communicate about each environment? By pervasive, I mean the typical feelings you continually experience in the course of your day.

For example, some people leave home in a great mood and spend all day at work in a state of frustration and anxiety. Others leave home feeling perturbed and become enthused once their team meeting has started, only to become dejected again shortly after dinner.

Everyone experiences distress at work and at home; that's a norm. However, when the pervasive mood you experience in these environments is distress, the emotional communication is saying you are not well off.

Reflect on the different emotions and moods that you experience in different environments and compare and contrast—you'll get some quick awareness into how some of your environments elicit different feelings in yourself—some positive, some not so positive.

In particular, in which environment, if any, do you *feel* distressed? How distressed? Mother Nature says your *high intensity* state of distress is urging you to move, or at the very least, to make adjustments.

Besides intensity, *length* of distressed time is important, too. When the distress message is calling you every day in a particular environment, it would be wise to make a move.

Everyday distress is a chronic condition, and, if it has been long term, you have spent a great deal of time already trying to adapt to the situation. Perhaps you are adapting and want to continue doing so. That is an individual choice. But be forewarned that people who choose to expose themselves to long-term distress, whether it is a marriage or a job, are never ones to thrive and feel as though they are living an enhanced live. How could they? There's too much distress.

Sometimes, the distress attributed to a particular environment is short-lived. Your partner's recovery from an illness might distress the whole family for weeks, but it inevitably passes. A company's physical renovation inconveniences everyone. But inevitably, the job is finished. An inexperienced manager is at the helm, but only for a month. A company suffers temporary difficulties because of temporary global events. In situations like this, it would be absurd to "shelter seek," because distress is known to be short-lived, so it is best to adapt to the temporariness of the situation, perhaps with the mental alternation: "It will soon be over."

On the other hand, if distress is intense and long term, your evolved natural instincts are telling you: *If you want to thrive, you have to leave a situation that you can only survive.* Chronic distress in an environment means move!

These two factors, *intensity* of distress and *length* of distress are vital communications. The degree of intensity tells you, "In this environment, you are really not doing well." The length of distress adds: "You've been feeling distressed for a while."

Put the distress messages together: "In this environment, you are not doing well, and it has been for a long time, so you better make a move if you want to do better."

Follow Your Emotions, Manage Them Not

When a lower creature is given the message of distress, it listens and makes the appropriate maneuver. It practices self-preservation.

The message for humans is that when you are given the long-term, chronic distress message; *do not* adhere to the conventional wisdom, to manage your emotions. Use strategic evolutionary psychology wisdom: *follow* your emotions.

Over the years, I've written several books on managing emotions and have counseled and taught thousands of people how to do just that. But I've come to question the enhancement value of managing emotions.

In effect, the conventional psychological wisdom behind managing emotions is that to do so will help you be more effective in all aspects of your life. Is this really true? A good case can be made that helping people manage their emotions is simply a way of helping them *adapt* to their situation, but paradoxically, it keeps them in the situation that inevitably was the source of their distress.

I've helped couples work out problems, so they could keep their marriage—for what purpose? So they could continue to work out their problems every week for the rest of their lives? I've helped top executives, seasoned managers, and line employees manage their emotions so that they could advance and stay in an organization that, for them, is the source of their frustration, anger, and anxiety. For these people, managing emotions in the conventional sense does not help them thrive; it only helps them survive by adapting.

I have reason to support this point. Studies investigating the responses to distressful events and environments show dominant responses that Mother Nature would classify as adaptive. A sample of responses would be making changes within yourself, so you can adapt such as lowering your expectations, trying to get over a problem, retreating from others, and even doing nothing. These responses simply help a person cope with the situation encountered.

Sure, there are times when managing your emotions is going to enhance the delivery of your presentation, your golf game, or your ability to help your children with their math problems when that does not come easy.

However, in chronic distressful environments, managing your emotions becomes paradoxical: It helps you stay in the situation by helping you adapt to it, to survive. You will *never* thrive because the environment does not provide you with what you need; the distress is the result of a *bad match* between you and the environment, be it your partner or your job.

Many animals have no choice but to adapt. But humans do have a choice. They can *adjust* and *seek out*. Switching jobs often enhances an individual's performance—the job environment is a better match, which is also true for the student who transfers to a different school and excels. Telling the student to remain in the same school and study harder, or to take a stress management class, is simply telling the student to adapt for the next four years when she could be thriving during that time.

"Follow through on your emotions!" is advice here. I've often wondered how many people would be in better marriages if I had encouraged them to listen to their distress and split up. Maybe a lot of them would be in marriages where the distress was once a month instead of every day. I wonder how many executives and employees would be thriving if I had guided them into exiting their job so they could get themselves into a work environment where their ideas are listened to with appreciation. I'd have to conclude that I've helped a lot of people stay in situations just so they could survive, not thrive.

I think the natural genius of your instincts could reverse the process so that more people could thrive. Instead of using your reasoning to help you adapt and survive, *use your innate hardwiring— your emotional distress—to guide your reasoning*. You might say: "This is a bad place for me, so it is smart for me to exercise my option to move on or make some adjustments." In fact, moving on or making adjustments is also part of the evolutionary function of distress: It motivates you to do something that reduces the distress and makes you feel better, to shelter seek.

As a clinician, I've found that acknowledging that a marriage or a job environment is not what you truly desire is a difficult reality for many people to confront. Why would this be so? Because an honest assessment might evoke shelter-seeking instincts, and because we are hardwired to be loss averse, anxieties and fears are aroused. Being dishonest to yourself keeps these anxieties and fears under control, but at the same time keeps you stuck in unhealthy environments and fosters instinctual disconnection.

Confronting the fact that your marriage and/or your job conditions are distressful does not mean that you have to leave them. You can make adjustments. But this is impossible to do if you are not honest in assessing the state of your environmental affairs.

Only you know how you really feel inside. Only you know if you are honestly answering questions such as these: Do *I feel good* about myself when I am with my husband, wife, or partner? Am I experiencing emotional growth in my relationship? Does my partner understand and respond to my needs? Does my partner encourage me to develop myself?

In my work environment, am I surrounded by people who encourage me? Does my job/work environment develop me? Do I feel secure in my work environment? Do I feel good when I am at work?

As I said, the key is to answer these questions with brutal honesty.

Home Sweet Home

Just as chronic distress tells you it's time to shelter seek, feelings of *joy*, *interest*, and *engagement* are the evolutionary barometers that tell you when you are in an environment that is empowering you to develop yourself, to be your best. When these feelings are the pervasive moods of the particular "environment," you know that you are in "Home, Sweet Home."

How you find your home is the subject of the next chapter.

3 ———————————

Home Hunting

To begin to connect to your shelter-seeking instincts, remember that their purpose is to guide you into the environment where you'll prosper and be happy.

From an evolutionary perspective, this means that the key variable in shelter seeking is *the interaction between the individual and the environment*. The more favorable the fit, the more empowering the environment will be to the individual. "I'm in a good place, I'm married to the right person, and I have the right job," are statements that communicate a good fit.

Emotional Nutrients

Whether Mother Nature is counseling a high school senior picking a university, a laid-off man or woman looking for that great, new job, a single person searching for "The One," or a company looking to relocate, Her question is going to be the same: "What are you looking for?" Without sarcasm, she would also tell you that if you can't answer this question, you are going nowhere fast. Indeed, the purpose of getting yourself in an empowering environment is to take advantage of what all humans are hardwired to do: *grow.*

Knowing *what makes you grow* is key to finding the right shelter—it's a crucial function of *self-awareness*, a popular term these days that has many meanings. For shelter-seeking instincts, self-awareness is your ability to know your *emotional nutrients*, what you need to develop to your potential.

Figuring out your needs doesn't have to cost you a lot of money in therapy, but it is one of those tasks that require time and honest self-evaluation. One strategy is writing in a journal. One terrific exercise is to complete these sentences:

"In my primary relation, to grow I need _____."
"In my job, to grow I need _____."

I've found that this topic is rarely discussed in performance appraisals, so describing what you need to grow at work might be a beneficial topic to discuss in your next review, if not sooner.

Be tuned in to the fact that we often hide from both ourselves and others the importance of our emotional and creative needs. When we fail to acknowledge what *really makes us feel good*, we foster instinctual disconnection, and the result, naturally, is to end up in an environment where we are ill-suited, one that makes us restless, dissatisfied, and miserable.

Why are many people resistant to expressing their true emotional incentives? Well, your evolutionary heritage suggests the fear of group rejection. Your ancestors, as you see later, depended on their clan for sheer survival. To go against the group, one would risk expulsion and lonely, risky exile, so conformity was a fundamental survival instinct. Similarly, the stock analyst who goes against the advice of the group risks being an outcast. So, instead, he goes along with conventional wisdom, even though his instincts are telling him that a million people can be wrong.

You have to be true to yourself when you state what you need from your partner or colleagues or boss. And, you will only know what you need after deep reflection and your willingness to accept truths about yourself. Self-awareness leads to authentic wisdom about the emotional nutrients *you* need.

Contentment Versus Growth

I've heard many people say that they are content in their jobs, content in their relationships. Contentment can be thought of as an adaptation. Its evolutionary value is that it helps individuals stay in an environment and, therefore, helps maintain relationships, families, and communities. The content wife stays in her "role." So does the "content" employee. Each goes through life with daily stresses, but neither is distressed. They are both content and, consequently, each has little desire to make a change.

Contentment is a pleasurable feeling, but it does not lead to growth and, in fact, often prevents growth. This is true for both individuals and organizations. Why might this be? Because contentment does not motivate you to move; rather it has the effect of keeping things the same. Since there are pleasurable feelings and minimum discomfort, there is no urge to make a change. Keeping things the same is the end result.

There is nothing wrong with keeping things the same, to be in a state of contentment if it is not hazardous to your well-being. But dozens of corporate case histories show that companies that are content inevitably become complacent and fall way behind the pack, some becoming extinct. Note that almost all great leaders you have met or read about rarely, if ever, have the attitude that they are content with their company's functioning. Rather, those individuals are always looking to make themselves and their organizations more effective, to strengthen their ecological niche.

As a psychologist, I would certainly say it is pretty good to feel content in your marriage, but what I also hope is that part of your contentment is that you feel that you are growing, that you are not just satisfied.

Remember, the purpose of shelter-seeking instincts is to help you get into an environment that empowers you to *continually grow so that you feel you are self-developing*. In today's world, that means a habitat that continually promotes your development. Moments of contentment are important for everybody, but pervasive contentment could be hazardous to your potential development.

It is also important to remember that is okay not to want to grow, to remain the same, to simply be content. But those who fall into this group are rarely those we think of as leaders.

Match Play, Nature's Course

An important point to acknowledge is that different work and relationship environments provide similar nutrients, although often to a significantly differing degree. All spouses might offer affection to each other, but the degree to which it is offered varies tremendously across couples. I've also observed that different work environments often provide totally different nutrients—such as physical setting, hours of operation, promotional opportunities, and financial incentives.

Individuals also have different needs that directly influence the type of environment they seek out. You may need to have a job that offers freedom in choosing job assignments, with financial incentives being significantly less important, while for another person, the opposite holds true. You may "need" a highly affectionate mate, while another man or woman prefers a less demonstrative one.

Finding the right match is crucial. The better the match between your emotional nutrients and those offered by the environment you seek (or are in), the more likely that you are putting yourself into an environment that will help you develop and establish your niche. An environment rich in nutrients might seem appealing, but if they are not in sync with your emotional nutrients, you best look elsewhere. To play well on Mother Nature's course, you have to be good at match play.

Your match play depends on the nature of the environment you are to assess, but a couple environmental nutrients are universal: *safety* and *security*.

Safety and security for your ancestors took their dominant form in the physical—having a shelter that would be difficult for other clans to access and having access to key resources yourselves. With these nutrients in place, the clan could begin to develop.

Today, safety and security take their form in emotion and feeling. Do you feel safe in disclosing your deep thoughts to your partner? Do you feel your partner is protective of you?

Think along the same lines in respect to your work environment. Are you genuinely encouraged to voice your thoughts, even to criticize your boss? Do you feel protected by your work colleagues?

Feeling safe and secure in your environment is empowering to your growth because it allows you to experiment with new behaviors (or products), and this newness is what leads to growth. A good action to take would be to generate some self-reflective questions that help you figure out how safe and secure you feel in your environments.

I've also become keenly aware that some environmental nutrients empower some people and yet are toxic to others. Some people, for example, flourish in a highly structured environment while others find the same environment stifling. They grow best with little structure. Many desire corporate cultures that are warm and fuzzy while I've worked with many individuals who prefer a nonpersonal environment. Some students find themselves in big universities while others need small classes in a small town to foster their development. Long before anyone else, Mother Nature sang, "Different strokes for different folks."

To ensure that you enter an environment that empowers you and to avoid one that is hazardous, you will do well to remember that shelter seeking is an active process: One of the ways you can make shelter seeking an active process is to scout your environment to be.

Scouting Your Environment

It's common practice for social insects to have *scouts* whose function is to seek out areas that contain favorable environmental elements, such as a bed of flowers for pollination. The scouts report back to the others, and if the news is good, others join the environment. Just like Christopher Columbus and Ponce de Leon, the scouts report and provide a "heads-up" of whether it makes sense for the group to immigrate to the new world.

Scouting out, or exploring a potential new environment, allows you to decide whether it's what you are looking for, whether its environmental nutrients are in tune with your core needs. Many people get themselves into mismatched settings because they do not give themselves an effective scouting report. They often rely on the scouting report of others and find out—too late—"I knew I never should have listened to him." "I should have visited the school personally instead of listening to my sister."

In our contemporary shelter-seeking exploratory efforts, our evolved instincts instruct us to focus on two variables that are interrelated: time and data.

Time

Time is the inherent evolutionary variable. Nothing evolves without its passage. From seconds to millions of years, evolution requires time. What is the function of evolutionary time?

Since evolution is defined by change, it must be to allow development to occur. All change and development has a time framework—sometimes seconds, sometimes hundreds of thousands of years. In either instance, change takes time. It takes time for a student to demonstrate progress, it takes time for an employee to do the same, and it takes time to develop real estate, natural or man-made. The length of time needed depends on the task that is to happen. For a fetus to develop into an infant, it takes nine months, whereas the development of man from earlier primates took hundreds of thousands of years.

No one can rush time. You might want the next 24 hours to pass quickly, but it is still going to take 24 hours. Sometimes, of course, time seems to take forever, or go extremely fast, but this is attributable to psychological perception, not the actual adjustment of physical time.

For proper instinctive shelter seeking, this means taking *enough* time to scout out your environment to be sure you make the right match play.

Data

If you've seen as many science fiction movies as I have, you know that when the space ship lands, step one is to analyze the atmosphere to see whether it will support life.

You need data about your environment—mainly; will it give you what you need to develop, to grow? Count on the fact that the caveman who first "analyzed" the components of his environment, to determine whether it was suitable to settle or better to keep on searching, was better at finding a home than his cousin who might have settled immediately because he liked the view only to realize too late that it was a long way from the market.

Most people hurt themselves by having data problems, either in the form of incomplete data or inaccurate data. Many times this occurs because not enough time was spent in data collection; other times we get ourselves into bad situations because we put our emphasis on inappropriate data, and this often happens when we are not tuned to our true emotional nutrients. Regardless, you need to search your environment for the data that helps you decide whether you are in the right place.

Sensing the Right Environment

You can take all the time you want and have all the data at your disposal, but you are still going to have to *sense and feel* whether it is the right environment for you. Don't be one of the people who equate *sensing* with having an intuitive gut feeling. Sensing is not a gut feeling. It is a hardwired tool—that your evolutionary instincts leverage to help you validate whether you are making the right choice.

Your senses enable you to process the world around you. Tuning in to the data your senses provide allows you to accurately decide whether the externals match up favorably with your internal feelings. In fact, it is the accuracy of this match that gives rise to sharp instincts.

Heighten and tune your awareness to sensory data and remember that what you see and hear is subject to your interpretation. You will always be better off when you can make sure your interpretations of the data are accurate by, for example, asking for clarification or collecting more data.

Seeing a lot of people sitting by themselves in a company cafeteria might give you a different instinctual sense than if you only listened to the recruiter telling you it's a "very interactive company culture." You might see a lot of people interested in what they are doing, but if you "hear" people say that instead it's a very competitive environment, your instincts might influence you a different way.

Mother Nature has given you multiple senses to learn about your environment. You need to remember to use *all* your senses to help assess whether the environment offers what you need. Naturally, what is needed is different for all of us, but it is hard to go wrong if you focus on an environment where you sense the potential of joy, interest, and engagement.

Interest motivates learning, the development of skills and competencies, and creative endeavor in a work environment, and fosters social bonds in a relationship. Whether it is a job or a partner, make

sure you *feel interested.* Make sure *"You're feeling it."* Joy is characterized by a sense of confidence, meaningfulness, and a feeling of
being loved and appreciated. Interest and joy create feelings of
engagement, best described as feeling productive and intellectually
and emotionally stimulated. These are your evolutionary barometers
for assessing whether your environment is empowering to you. The
more intensely and frequently you feel them, the truer the match.

Bring this self-awareness and emotional listening to every shelter-
seeking effort—a new office, a new community, a new person. What
do you *see* that you like and dislike? What *excites* you? What do you
see that *interests* you? What do you *hear*? What are the positives that
are said and the negatives, too? How does the environment *feel*? Do
you feel *engaged, interested, and excited*? In other words, the more
you see and hear, the more you will sense and feel if this environment
could be Home Sweet Home, right where you belong.

Using your senses to gather and analyze data is essential to any
shelter seeking effort. How we use data, what kind we need, and the
time needed to sharpen our shelter-seeking instincts varies based on
the type of environment you seek. The next chapter illustrates examples of how you can apply these concepts in your own life.

4 ———————————

Shelter Seeking Today

Getting yourself into an empowering environment, as stated earlier, is mandatory for having an enhanced life, and those who are in empowering environments will surely vouch for this, as will those who aren't.

In your daily life, there are plenty of times when taking advantage of your shelter-seeking instincts makes your life better, ranging from finding the right mate, getting the right job, empowering your environments, and even leaving a nightmarish relationship—all scenarios covered here.

The Job Interview/Selection/Promotion/Transfer

What's your goal on a job interview? The common response is the obvious one: "To get the job." Yet, every year, the young, and even the seasoned, get themselves into the wrong environment by getting the job.

Shelter-seeking instincts here instruct you to have a different goal, at least initially, and that is to *scout* the environment—to get a feel for all the forces that will impact you.

Part of a job interview is to show off your abilities. But for too many people, this is their lone job interview focus. To shelter seek effectively, take the perspective that the job interview is *your* time to scout the environment, to see if it is the right Environment of Evolutionary Adaptedness for you, not if you are right for the job. *Interview the job.* This means you have to be much more active in the interview process; otherwise, you will not gain the data you need to make a choice that is in your best interest. The same holds true before you accept a new position—whether upstairs or across the country.

I remember a college senior, an English major, who was thrilled that she got a job as a junior editor for a technical magazine. Her goal was to become a novelist, and she reasoned that becoming an editor would be helpful and further her understanding of the creative process and good writing. She had sent the magazine her transcripts, recommendations, samples of her work from the school newspaper, and had a "great phone interview," she told me. With great expectations, she happily took the job. A week later, she found that the type of work she was doing was boring her to death. If only she had asked for an example of the *task data*, the type of writing she would be editing. She could have quickly come to the conclusion that this job was not going to give her what she needed. Note there is a big difference between being *told* what type of work you will be doing and actually *seeing* the type of work you will be doing.

Gather the data you need to make a choice that is in your best interest. *See* and *feel* the *people data*—ask to meet the people you will be working with, especially the person who will be supervising you and don't be shy about *interviewing that person.* Check out the *physical data*, space you will be working in, to see if it is to your liking. Ask for examples of potential job assignments so that you can see if the job tasks are *interesting* to you, an emotional job nutrient for sure.

If you lack the clout to "demand" this data in the formal job interview, seek it informally, like the new graduate with an MFA in fashion marketing who walked through all the major upscale department stores and, posing as a customer, initiated conversations with employees so that she could *hear* their thoughts and feelings about her potential work environment. This gave her valuable data to help her find the type of environment that would promote her.

Evaluate your data thoughtfully. What is most important for the purpose of helping you grow? Be honest here or suffer the consequences. Also, some nutrients take longer to have their impact on you than others. A supportive environment in the short run might do little for your growth but put you in a much better position two years down the road. You will grow. On the other hand, another environment might start you out with greater compensation with an immediate impact on your life style. Two years later, though, you feel your career going nowhere fast. Sometimes, we have to choose some nutrients at the expense of others, and the advice here is to always seek the one that helps you grow. It is a sound idea to prioritize your emotional nutrients and see how the job environment stands on providing them.

The same is true for internal transfers, such as a promotion that requires a physical relocation. "Look before you leap," is the evolutionary driven caution. At first glance it might look like a great opportunity, but the more you look, the less you like it. Again, taking a long look requires time.

Whether you are entering the work force or seeking a new job, a new position, your choice is sure to have major consequences in your life. The message of shelter seeking here is to stay on the right path by gathering as much *environmental data* as possible, so you can see if you not only match up, but more importantly, if it's an environment that will encourage your growth for years to come.

College Selection

Every year, the college selection process becomes more prevalent in America, and every year, tens of thousands of students are ready to transfer after their first year on the grounds they made the wrong choice.

If you are the parent of a college-bound student, encourage the student to shelter seek for the right college environment, one that will help the student grow. Before you spend a lot of time and money with a college counselor, spend the time to follow Mother Nature's advice to help your college-bound student arrive at the choice through the use of his or her *own* shelter-seeking instincts.

First you have to *help college bound students tune in to their emotional nutrients, not their SAT scores.* Do this by having frequent conversations centered on their *interests*, their *aspirations*. Get them to think about some college logistics—the size of the school, geographical locations, and most importantly, what they want a school *to offer them.* Too many parents and their children focus on "what are the best schools I can get into," whereas the concept of shelter seeking says your selection will be better when you focus on seeking schools that can offer you what you need—special help, financial assistance, nutrients that might not be available from one of the "best schools you can get into." In other words, the best school a college-bound student can get into is not necessarily the right school. Shelter seeking tells you to help your son or daughter pick the *right* school, not necessarily the best school.

Studying brochures and speaking to college advisors and college counselors are useful activities, but to help children maximize *their* shelter-seeking instincts, encourage them to experience, to *feel* the environments they are thinking of entering for the next four years of their life.

More than just walking the campus and going on the morning or afternoon tour, encourage your kids to do more, such as attending a class, visiting a friend who goes to the school and spending the night, or eating meals with other students. You get the idea—you want to help your son or daughter sense the environment by getting them to *see*, *hear*, and *feel* the college environment he or she is considering, and this is best done by spending time in the environment, not just visiting it.

Next, interview them about their college visits, your goal being to help them clarify their feelings and thoughts about their experience. Make sure you ask them to *compare* and *contrast* the experiences of their visits, how they felt with and about the other kids, impressions of class difficulty, the college town itself. Use the sensory questions: "What did you *see* that you liked and interested you? What did you *hear* your friends and other students say? How did you *feel* being there?" Answers to these questions help your college-bound child assess whether he or she is making a smart match play. Remember, feeling interested, engaged, and joy are cues your son or daughter are entering an empowering environment.

Shelter seeking for the right college environment is a time-consuming process, but it is well worth it since the right environment helps your children grow.

Mating: Love and Business

Wolves are the number one predator in North America. They have a strong ecological niche, but they are rarely the love birds that inspire poets. Yet, they mate for life, something that is rare among humans. Similarly, female prairie voles—those little rodents with the devoted male partners—require extensive contact with a would-be mate before they become sexually receptive.

How do you select the right mate? Nobody knows, but perhaps we can learn something from wolves and voles that increases the likelihood that we do; and that is: When it comes to selecting a mate, take your time.

Compared to Mother Nature's other creatures, wolves, Mr. and Miss Canis Lupus have a long courting period. For a wolf, time is of the essence, but for them essence means spending a lot of time is essential to selecting the right mate.

To select the right mate, whether it is a person, a business partner, or a company to merge with, you have to know the nutrients they provide, and if they are the nutrients that will help you grow. You have to scout. To do this effectively requires time, lots of it.

In selecting a personal mate, time affords you the opportunity to uncover the true nature of the environment you might enter. Use your senses to collect the data, such as seeing how the person reacts to you in stressful situations. How does he deal with conflict and time apart? Does she support your need for alone time and time you may want to spend apart from her to be with your friends and family? This might not be apparent until you have known the person for many months, not several weeks. The same is true for perceiving certain beliefs and values, forces that might impede your growth but are not apparent in the initial shelter-seeking weeks.

You might require support nutrients and, at first, this environment seems to provide it. However, a good time later, when you really need support, it is nowhere in sight. Put simply, for best mate selection, Mother Nature recommends to her sons and daughters a long engagement period.

During this time, your shelter-seeking task is to relate to the environment in an intimate manner. The data to gather are *thoughts* and *feelings*, so this means the plentiful sharing of thoughts and feelings. Unfortunately, as many therapists will tell you, many people are ill at ease when comes to sharing their thoughts and feelings. Thoughts and feelings are risky data to share because they tap into your feelings of vulnerability. Yet, these risky forms of communication are the tools that allow you to know each other and discover whether you will support each other through sickness and health, richer or poorer, or lead to an anguishing divorce.

Recall that one of the environmental nutrients that help us all is safety and security. You can see one of the reasons this is true. The safer and more secure you feel, the more likely you are to disclose your own thoughts and feelings and solicit those of others. Thus, a good cue to help you decide whether your shelter seeking is taking you down the right path is *how comfortable you feel in disclosing your thoughts and feelings* during the engagement period and how comfortable the other person is in doing the same. And a follow-up self-help tip would be to get comfortable in disclosing your thoughts and feelings, since these will always be good tools to help discover the emotional nature of any interpersonal environment you enter.

The same is true for selecting a business partner. Quickly formed partnerships usually don't last and often end in a lawyer's office. Spending a lot of time with prospective business partners affords you the opportunity to assess the traits that you need to make business go. We all know that what the person brings to the table on paper can be deceiving. Only by spending time with the person behind the paper will you be able to make the right selection. Business meetings, sports activities, dinners, and phone conversations are all ways to spend time with prospective business partners to find out if they are a suitable match for you.

Empowering Your Environment

Where you are right now—in home and work—might be far from empowering, and with your hardwiring to be loss averse, you're not leaving. Don't despair, because you can still create a happy ending by empowering your environment, or at least make it less than a taxing shelter.

Your capacity to interact and influence your environment is what allows you to adjust your shelters from ones that impede your growth to ones that empower it.

Mother Nature tells you that you must have an environment that provides you with the emotional nutrients that feed your growth. So, in your intimate relationships, the urge to shelter seek signals that the *emotional nutrients*, yours and your partners, are not being met; that's why you feel like looking elsewhere. A partner who does not know what emotional nutrients you need cannot provide them, and thus, cannot help you grow. In effect, you have to create *emotional environmental awareness* in your partner.

An easy exercise can help. Sit with your partner and both take 30 minutes to make a list of your most important emotional nutrients. Then, each of you is to make a list of what you think your partner's most important emotional nutrients are and how you feel they could be added into the relationship. Then review your list and share your thoughts and feelings.

I've used this exercise many times in counseling couples and in relationship workshops and have found that when partners are aware of each other's emotional nutrients, they can make adjustments and better attend to them. When partners do this, the relationship is empowered—both partners feel relationship growth, and this feeling continues to fuel the empowerment of the relationship. Naturally, there is no guarantee, but the situation is helped if both partners earnestly want to empower their relationship.

Note that your tools to implement the preceding exercise are feeling comfortable in disclosing your thoughts and feelings to your partner (otherwise, you will never speak about your true emotional nutrients) and a willingness to listen to their thoughts and feelings.

What about being in a job environment where going to work is literally going to work? Again, if you are going to stay and want to do more than survive, you have to remember your evolutionary heritage and be an active force so you can empower your job, not vice versa.

Begin like always—clarify the emotional nutrients that you need and identify those that are not provided. Next, practice the communication skill of assertiveness when expressing your thoughts and feelings in a socially appropriate manner. This translates to you taking the initiative of meeting with your supervisor/manager/boss and explaining your job feelings—more or less, saying, "I do not feel I am growing in my job." Then, assert what you feel you need to grow on the job—the type of experiences, job assignments, managerial style, that you feel will bring to life the emotional nutrients you need. This practice is no guarantee that you will get what you need, but countless executives and managers who have followed this procedure have found they can turn their job around to the point that they actually enjoy going to work.

Similarly, I've conducted numerous company retreats and found that taking time for senior executives to address their emotional nutrients, the emotional nutrients of their teams, and the emotion nutrients of employees in general leads to management that is much more likely to have a better bottom line, and not surprisingly, a work force characterized by high retention of key talent and a positive morale. These folks realize that empowerment means more than letting others make decisions and have greater responsibility; to them it means helping them express their human nature to "emotionally grow" on the job. Helping things grow is one of Mother Nature's job tasks.

The Great Escape: Leaving the Nightmare

It is a dilemma that millions face—can't adjust, can't leave, are sick of adapting, but just can't get out of a relationship or a job. There's a lot of clinical jargon to describe individuals who are in *that* situation, but for the most part, it's pretty useless in helping these folks move on to enhancement. Plus, many of these people fill the calendars of therapists only to find that they still wake up with misery. What do you do?

You will not hear this advice from any therapist, unless, of course she has been trained in strategic evolutionary therapy by Mother Nature. You don't have to slip out the back, Jack, or get a new key, Lee, and you don't have to get on a bus, Gus, but you do need to mix the evolutionary function of emotions, namely, anger, disgust, contempt. And fear.

Since you have probably been stuck a long time (you're hardwired to stay), I'll give you a fast recipe to get out. First, you need some anger. In the evolution of human beings, anger was important for survival. Its value lay in its ability to *mobilize* one's energy and make one capable of defending oneself with great vigor and strength. Though not known to be a universal cause, a common stimulus to anger is the feeling of being either physically or psychologically restrained from doing what one intensely desires to do—which in this case, is leaving a dead-end dysfunctional relationship or a job. You need some *anger arousal* so you can mobilize the energy that will be required to walk out the door. Thus, *increase* your thoughts pertaining to how frustrated you are in your environment, how it stops you from expressing your potential. "I'm angry and I'm not going to take it anymore!" would be one of your *motivational statements to leave*.

At the same time, use your angry face: Use the muscles of your brow to move them inward and downward; this creates a frown and foreboding appearance around your eyes. It is probably hard to dilate your nostrils so that the wings of your nose flare out, but you can keep your lips open and drawn back in a rectangle like shape revealing your clinched teeth. When your face flushes red, you are doing excellent, but don't go overboard and bring it to a boil—just keep it at a simmer to give you some fuel for action.

Now, throw in some *disgust*. Closely related to anger, things that are deteriorated or spoiled, either organically or psychologically, cause disgust. Disgust evolved from the hunger drive and the behavior associated with it. Thus, the blueprint of a disgusting situation is something that "tastes bad." If you need a face, the image is of one of gagging or spitting out, with the pulling upward of the upper lip, a wrinkling of the nose, and eyes that appear to be squinting—like you've just bitten into a rotten lemon.

When something disgusts us, we want to remove it or change it in such a way that it is no longer disgusting. In evolution, disgust probably helped motivate organisms to maintain an environment sufficiently sanitary for their health, prevented them from eating spoiled food and drinking polluted water, and played a role in the maintenance of body hygiene. Foul body odors or a grossly dirty appearance may be disgusting to the self and others; failure to clean up the environment may prove disastrous for the group, and failure to maintain body cleanliness that meets the group's standards may lead to rejection and isolation.

To take advantage of disgust, start to ruminate on how disgusting your relationship is or your job and work environment. Focus on how it has deteriorated, spoiled to the point that it "stinks." Remind yourself that such disgust is unacceptable for your mental hygiene, and the bottom line is that it is so disgusting you have to get rid of it, just like a terrible body odor.

Very important—do not let the disgust turn the anger into a boil. The idea is to use your anger to give you the energy to rid yourself of something that is toxic to you, and if the anger boils, it will motivate you to act counterproductively.

With anger and disgust, you are walking to the door, but to keep going, add some *contempt*. This shouldn't be difficult to do because contempt often occurs with anger or disgust or with both.

Contempt may have evolved as a vehicle for preparing the individual or group to face a dangerous adversary. Today, the situation in which the individual has a need to feel superior—stronger, more intelligent, more civilized, more mentally healthy—may lead to some degree of contempt. Importantly for your purpose, contempt is a "cold" emotion, one that tends to depersonalize the individual or group held in contempt. Accordingly, it can motivate tough, even cruel acts. For you, leaving your environment is a tough act, and at times, might even seem as if you are being self-centered and cruel. That's why you need contempt, to defeat any guilt and remorse that could pull you back if you let them linger.

Have contempt by focusing on the fact that leaving the situation is the only civilized thing to do, and that you are only able to do this because of your superior moral fiber. Be proud that you have the ability to be cold-hearted when needed. To get the look, cock your eyebrows, stretch your face, and keep your head lifted up so that you give the appearance that you are looking down on someone. You will find that this expression of contempt also gives the impression that you are pulling away, creating distance between you and the other, which is exactly what you want.

These three emotions—anger, disgust, and contempt—have been termed the *hostility triad* and naturally would not be helpful if you wanted to stay in your current situation. But, since you want out, they are exactly what you need. They get you to the door. As your final push, give yourself a sprinkling of *fear.*

Fear affects all human beings, and at one time or another it leaves its mark on each of us. Fear is the most toxic of all the emotions. Intense fear can even kill. Animals, including human beings, are sometime literally frightened to death.

Yet fear is not all bad. It serves as a danger warning signal that redirects thought and action. From an evolutionary-biological perspective, fear can be adaptive and facilitate social bonds by releasing *flight to one another* and contributing to a collective defense.

You don't need too much fear—just enough to remind you that you are in a dangerous situation and you need to "flee." Accomplish this by imagining what your life will be like if you continue to stay put. *Your entire existence will be threatened, and you will not survive— your only chance is to leave.* Perhaps visualizing your relationship or job as a horrific monster will help you get the *feel* of fear.

Remember, you are hardwired to stay, so the thought of leaving is often anxiety arousing. Anxiety often creates thoughts of uncertainty, and you end up staying in the situation, uncertain about what to do. If you can give yourself just enough fear, it will help you override your anxiety and walk through the door with the knowledge that whatever is on the other side will be better than what you are leaving.

To have the look, make believe your relationship or job is a monster that is front of you. Your look is eyes wide open, eyebrows are approximately straight and appear somewhat raised, the inner corners of your brow are drawn together, and there are horizontal wrinkles that extend across three quarters of your forehead. Your lower eyelid is tensed, and your upper eyelid slightly raised.

Give yourself help by frequently mixing up these emotions every day, and for good measure, make the appropriate facial expressions, too. This will all help get you in the perfect frame of mind and the right mood to do what you have been unable to do—leave.

Anger, disgust, contempt, and fear—that's the way you go, Joe!

The Future of Shelter Seeking

Scientists are in agreement that it is only a matter of time before Earth becomes uninhabitable for humans. No doubt, by the time that happens, we will have the technology to help us shelter seek throughout the universe. When that time comes, how well we shelter seek will determine the future of our success.

Part II

Care Solicit...So You Can Protect Your Vulnerabilities

Enhance your life by using your care soliciting instincts

5

Protecting Your Vulnerabilities

Your Evolutionary Heritage

A blackbird chick drops a wriggling worm from its tiny beak. It scrambles in the grasses of its nest but is too uncoordinated as yet to pick up the worm from the twig it is under. It begins to make cheeping noises while holding his head up in the air with a gaping beak. Quickly the mother flies back to her nest to help her chick.

911

The cheeping noise from the baby blackbird is an example of a behavior whose function is a call for care and attention. You might think of this as *infantile behavior*, but in the most successful species, it is called *care soliciting* and is thought to be a mature behavior. In the animal world, the call for help arises in situations where an animal cannot solve the problem itself, so it raises a call or signal for care and attention from another animal in its family group.

The Cry for Help Gets a Helping Hand

Imagine that, back on the Savannah, one of your ancestors who is just a few thousand years down from the trees wanders off to explore. He stumbles into a pit. He tries, but he can't jump or climb out. He cries for help and soon enough another early man comes to rescue him, by reaching down and pulling him out. Maybe this was the original cry for help as well as the reaching out of a helping hand. Your ancestors who developed the *adaptation to ask for help* when in a vulnerable situation increased their chances for survival, and this instinctual tool got passed down to us today.

This evolutionary adaptation has a critical function—to help you protect your vulnerabilities. The below average student who asks for help to protect his or her vulnerability in biology is being smart. Employees who ask their managers for help in developing their skills are the ones who develop to their fullest. The couple who asks for each other's help *will* enhance their marriage.

Asking for help is part of your human nature, an adaptation ingrained into your bio-physiology. We have numerous internal organs and systems that, if running sub par, send out a signal for help. One example is the endocrine system, particularly the thyroid gland. When the gland is not producing sufficient thyroid hormones to keep the body's metabolism running efficiently, a signal is sent to the pituitary gland. It responds by producing a hormone that travels back to stimulate production of thyroid hormones. In effect, one gland asks another for help and gets it.

Even before a baby sees the light, it has already established a complex communication system in which it is able to signal to its mother's body to meet its needs. Upon birth, the infant's facial expressions, and vocalizations continue the function that communicates to the mother, "I am vulnerable and I need you to help me," and these communications help the infant survive.

Yet, as we grow into adulthood, the instinct to ask for help seems to be inhibited. The world is filled with presidents, CEOs, managers, and front line employees who have all failed because they did not ask for help; the same holds true for students at all levels of education. It is also true that many marriages suffer because partners do not follow their natural instinct to request the support of each other.

Why is care soliciting, even when we know we need it and when it is the natural action to take, so often ignored?

Vulnerability: Positive Feelings-Not

Vulnerability is an important evolutionary concept that refers to anything that puts a creature at risk, makes a threat to its survival. The vulnerability could be part of its nature—for example, a creature's slowness, which puts it at risk to a faster predator. Or the vulnerability could be part of the environment, such as the drying up of a water hole.

Similarly, an executive's demeanor could be his or her personal vulnerability, while a drying up of capital like the water hole could be an external vulnerability. Whether internal or external, the creatures that can quickly identify and protect their vulnerabilities will have an edge, and thus be favored by natural selection.

We all are born with vulnerabilities, and it also follows that we are all programmed to make efforts to protect those vulnerabilities; just like the blackbird chick, we cannot survive without the aid of others.

Vulnerability is part of human nature, but I've found that few people like to acknowledge it. In speaking to a group of several hundred husbands and wives, I asked: "How many of you like to *feel* vulnerable?" A few days later, I asked the same question in a classroom filled with executives. I know that you will not be surprised to hear that not one person in either group raised his or her hand, although there were a lot of laughs.

People don't like to feel vulnerable. Why should this be so? The answer from the standpoint of your evolutionary heritage is that vulnerability is a natural stimulant for unpleasant feelings of anxiety and fear.

Anxiety Disorders

Back on the savannah, it was a perilous time, and survival was won every day. It was an era when an individual's vulnerability or a group's vulnerability literally could lead to death. To help protect these vulnerabilities, to bring them to the awareness of the individual so that they could respond to the threat message and act to resolve the threat, Mother Nature evolved anxiety and fear. These emotions have the evolutionary function of *warning you of a threat.*

Note that in the time of your ancestors, vulnerabilities were predominantly of the *physical* domain: speed of a creature, comparative strength in an individual (making a weak individual "vulnerable" to doing poorly in the hunting party), unstable climatic and geological forces. These vulnerabilities all *threatened the physical life* of an individual and the clan. Back then, anxiety was not just a nervous disorder, it meant the difference between life and death. It aided early man to survive in a hazardous environment because these emotions warned the individual to be on guard. Indeed, anxiety would help change disorder to order.

As the eons passed, the world became safer for humankind, but the anxiety and fear instinct remained intact. The invention of agriculture, for example, greatly diminished the risk of a drought-killed food supply, a major vulnerability in the hunter-gatherer era. Agriculture created food surplus, so there was diminished need to be anxious or fearful that the clan would starve to death. Similarly, as climates stabilized, some predators became extinct. Humankind invented strong shelters, more effective weapons, and advanced defense tactics. As the world became safer, the survival function of intense fear and anxiety instincts lessened, but this adaptation, nonetheless, was passed down intact to modern women and men.

Vulnerability Today

Our thoughts and behavior evolved because they served a purpose in the environment in which we once operated, an environment radically different from that in which we live today.

The mismatch between our caveman level of fear and anxiety and our relatively secure world today is known in evolutionary psychology parlance as a *maladaptation*. It's the cause for many of the neuroses and some of the psychoses that are too common today.

We are still susceptive to physical vulnerabilities—earthquakes, hurricanes, tornadoes, environmental pollution, global warming, poor health—but there is no modern need to make giant leaps from one rock to another or to swim through the East river in search of food. The problem is, though, that many people feel the same intensity of anxiety and fear that cavemen did.

An executive who learns that her demeanor might be an impediment to a promotion is apt to become anxious at work when presented with that information since, in her mind, this vulnerability threatens her corporate survival. A student becomes maladaptively anxious about his D in chemistry because in his mind, it threatens his dream of becoming a veterinarian. In both these situations, the individual experiences threat on a *primal* level. The intensity is disproportionate to the situation and exacerbates the problem.

Your charging boss might seem to be attacking you, and while his words may seem scratching and biting to you, and you might spill your "emotional blood," the fact is, it's not the same as being charged by a Saber tooth tiger. Your thoughts can create ulcers and migraines, but even so, the damage is done by your "reason," not the physical reality as in the case of your ancestors.

Accordingly, when we consider the fact that there is a high rate of diagnosed clinical anxiety disorders that cut across gender, income, and occupation, and add to that the number the people who test just below diagnosable, our evolutional heritage manifests and confirms itself since many people become intensely anxious when they have to confront their weaknesses.

How do *you* deal with *feeling* vulnerable, and how does it affect your ability to use your care-soliciting instincts?

The Invulnerability Trap

In evolutionary psychology, fear and anxiety are your pals because they alert you to the need to protect yourself. Evolutionary psychologists work with emotions by studying their *expressive* function. Thus, they use the face as their hardwiring apparatus; a fearful face would express to another that the two of you might be vulnerable.

In contrast, clinical and counseling psychologists focus on the *experience* of emotion—the feelings component, often thought to be the distinguishing characteristic of human nature.

While sometimes fear and anxiety can be perceived as pleasurable and even desirable—horror movies, gambling, extreme sports are just a few examples—most people hate these feelings. Few people report that their day was great because they felt worried. Few husbands and wives look forward to getting home so that they can feel dread or terror!

From my clinical and coaching activities, I've found that all too often most people are overwhelmed by these emotions, since they are using a maladaptive response to the "vulnerability" of the situation.

For our ancestors, one of the best ways to deal with their anxieties was to physically escape it—running like hell, or finding a protected cave on high ground and keeping the fire burning all night to scare away the beasts. Their anxiety instinct motivated protective action. The action responded to the threat, and the fear diminished. *Feeling* the anxiety and the fear gave your ancestors an edge.

Today, we experience emotional vulnerability—defined as feelings of weakness or a sense of feeling threatened. But if the vulnerability is part of your nature, physically leaving won't work. An employee can quit before she is fired, but she will take her angry nature with her. A student whose study habits make him vulnerable to poor grades can transfer to another school, but the poor study habits are still his roommate.

Not being able to physically escape the threat of vulnerability, modern humans all too often deal with emotional or situational vulnerabilities by *psychologically* escaping—pretending that they are invulnerable. They suppress their distressing feelings.

In action, an executive/manager/employee finds acknowledging his abrasive personality to be anxiety arousing because it would force him to confront that his demeanor is a risk to his career. These thoughts become so uncomfortable that the executive/manager/ employee reduces them by either getting defensive, becoming argumentative, or ignoring what he is told. Or he chooses to believe that the vulnerability is insignificant. All of these denials serve the purpose of helping the executive/manager/employee *psychologically escape* the discomfort of anxiety.

An evolutionary perspective would help the executive/manager/ employee see that his denial prevents him from using the evolved function of the anxieties—the message that risk is in the air—so ACT! He doesn't act, and the threat doesn't go away. It's like ignoring your next door neighbor's shouts: "Your house is on fire!"

Thoughts About Asking

Asking for help is uncomfortable because it makes us feel vulnerable and thus arouses anxieties, fears, and a feeling of weakness. Making it even more difficult is that many of the messages that stem from popular mental health and corporate wisdom prevent people from asking for help when they need it most. See if your thoughts match up to these care-soliciting inhibiting thoughts. They all provide an example of how ruling with reason hurts rather than helps.

Independence = Emotional Health

It is one thing to ask somebody for a ride when your car is at the mechanic or to ask someone to do a simple favor for you, but it is a different matter to ask someone for help when you are feeling down and out.

As long as I can remember, a popular message from the genre of self-help books is that it is emotionally healthy to be independent. So prevalent is this message that many people do not ask for help because they think doing so would be an admission that they are emotionally ill, which would do irreparable harm to their standing. Thus, people try to solve their problems by themselves, even to the point that not solving them leads to stress and depression.

Any psychologist will tell you that calling on your own "resilience" to bounce back from setbacks and cope with problems is a hallmark of the emotionally healthy person. But it is also a hallmark of the emotionally healthy to ask for help when they need it. Indeed, as you see later, you are hardwired to be dependent on others.

A plethora of research indicates that individuals with good self-esteem view asking others for help as one of the attributes that make them successful. Similarly, people who do best in rebounding from job setbacks are those who reach out for help from others, from talking about their anger and depression to phoning former colleagues to find out who's hiring. The same is true for people who cope best with the news of a medical catastrophe—they share their fears with loved ones and/or a support group.

Are You Incompetent?

"I don't ask for help because, at my level, the expectation is that I know what to do. If ask for help, it's saying I am incompetent." This might seem like an extreme and distorted thought, but the fact is, that 30 other vice presidents in the Wharton School class nodded their heads in agreement when one person voiced this opinion.

I've discovered that a common reason people do not solicit help is their deep belief that others will interpret it as a sign of incompetence—a perception that would put the "asker" at risk. I've found this thinking to be prevalent at all levels of occupational status but dramatically more so at management and executive levels.

The working world has actually done a lot to create this belief. Thirty years of labels such as "entrepreneur," "peak performer," "maverick," "renegade," and "decisive decision maker" all revere the Western ideal of the self-reliant man or woman. Even in reality shows, we see that the contestants who show they need the help of others are typically voted off, and those who take charge stay in the game. No one wants to be seen as "the weakest link."

But solid research indicates that star performers in organizations are those who seek the help of others. They call on the strengths of their team. They are tuned in to using their care-soliciting instincts.

The Fear of Refusal

One young couple was experiencing some typical marital stress. The one issue surfacing in a session centered on their finances. The husband was upset because his wife refused to ask her parents to help them with the down payment for their first house. The husband was particularly angry because his parents had given them plenty, and he knew that his in-laws had money to spare. Yet, his wife persisted with, "I don't want to ask them. They don't have it. They give in other ways. They need it for themselves."

By the end of the session, with the help of some gentle exploration of her feelings, it became apparent that her real hesitation was her fear that her parents would say, "NO!" That they would refuse her the care she requested and needed.

Many people do not solicit care because they are inhibited by the fear that they will be refused. For these people, the act of being refused by a friend or parent is a tough pill to swallow. After all, a refusal is typically not what we expect from a friend, let alone a parent.

In these cases, the culprit that prevents care soliciting is the "reason"—the belief that a refusal is *equivalent* to "You don't care about me." In the preceding case, her parents' refusal would have been interpreted as, "You don't love me." By not asking for help, she would not have to deal with the possibility of being refused and feeling hurt, unloved, and rejected.

An important point to remember here is that while you are hardwired to solicit care, it does not mean you will always get the assistance you ask for. Moreover, interpreting a refusal as "They don't care" is far from rational. People give refusals for all sorts of reasons, many having nothing to do with their level of care toward you. Many parents, for example, refuse to help their children on the grounds that "It's time for you to stand on your own two feet." The issue is not whether this parental reason is flawed, but rather, it has nothing to do with their love for their children.

In short, holding the belief that a refusal signals a lack of care, concern, and commitment is irrational, what most clinical psychologists would consider a *neurotic belief*. And it prevents you from using your care soliciting instincts.

Note the irony of these messages. Humans are hardwired to ask for help when they need it, but contemporary messages tell us to suppress our human nature—to be self-reliant, independent, solve your own problems, sink or swim on your own efforts. Acting on these beliefs, whether on the Savannah or on Wall Street, is the opposite of what Mother Nature intended, and thus, you handicap yourself. You create a mismatch by preventing your natural instincts from acknowledging you need help.

6

The Benefits of Vulnerability

In my years of working with people, I've found Mother Nature's advice to be sound. Individuals, couples, families, and organizations who acknowledge their vulnerabilities benefit because *acknowledging their vulnerability allows them to ask for help*.

An individual who recognizes a job deficiency is more apt to seek out help to improve than one who is defensive. A couple who confront their feelings that their marriage is vulnerable to divorce is more likely to take action to resolve their problems. Parents who acknowledge that their teenagers are vulnerable to substance abuse give themselves the opportunity to help their kids rise above it.

Organizations that are quick to identify their vulnerabilities increase their speed and effectiveness for dealing with them and thus, nip problems in the bud. This is why many organizations continually and formally assess their vulnerabilities.

The important and useful point here is that Mother Nature has created an adaptation for protecting vulnerabilities—asking for help, or as she would put it, *care soliciting*.

To tap into your evolutionary heritage, to take advantage of your care-soliciting instincts, to escape the trap of invulnerability, you first have to do what your ancestors did: You have to allow yourself to *feel* vulnerable, or more broadly, *feel comfortable in feeling vulnerable*.

Befriending Your Feelings

Befriending your feelings is another one of those concepts that can be streamlined into a page or two, but in reality takes several months for you to realize fruitful gains, assuming you are diligent in your efforts. As you befriend your feelings in general, it becomes easier to befriend specific feelings, such as the feeling of vulnerability.

Your task is to get comfortable with the experiential component—the *feelings* of vulnerability (anxiety, weaknesses), so you can take advantage of their communicative evolutionary function: a cue that you are at risk so that you can and should *do* something about it. When you are comfortable with these feelings, you can confront the reality of the risk and deal with it effectively rather than denying its existence due to feeling discomfort.

Most therapists would agree that as a person becomes more accepting of her vulnerabilities, she becomes less likely to try to hide them; rather she becomes more comfortable in understanding them and looking for productive ways to diminish them. The end result is a more enhanced individual.

You can initiate the process of befriending your feelings by becoming *more aware* of them. Be your own best friend here and practice self-help. It's an effort, but keeping a Feeling Journal can benefit you. At the end of the day or at different times of the day, make a note of what feelings you have experienced in the preceding hours. This reconnects you with your awareness of how and what you feel each day.

Analyze your journal. What feelings do you experience the most? When are you angry, happy, sad? Think about the messages these feelings gave you and how you responded to these warnings.

Increase your awareness of feelings by paying attention to the *physical feels* you have every day; give yourself assignments to touch something smooth, soft, and hard. Studies show that as physical sensitivities increase, so do psychological sensitivities. Remember, your ancestors learned a lot about the world simply through physical sensations. You might feel the pain when a competitor takes a "bite" out of your business, but your ancestors actually felt the bite. In other words, the physical sensations that we get from touch are frequently transferred into psychological feelings. Bad news might *numb* you, but you were first familiarized with the feeling of numbness through the physical sensations of your foot falling asleep, or Novacaine from your dentist.

Another activity is to practice expressing your feelings, simply by stating periodically throughout the day, "I feel _____." Acknowledge your feelings and feel more comfortable with them. Say the statement out loud when you are by yourself, or, if your comfort level permits, in the presence of others, like your partner and colleagues.

Practicing these activities with diligence will help you feel more comfortable with feeling vulnerable, a necessity for getting yourself to care solicit.

Be a Small Risk Taker

Learn how to feel vulnerable by taking small risks in which the consequences aren't harmful. Going to an unfamiliar restaurant might make you vulnerable to paying for a bad meal, but it is not going to kill or bankrupt you. Taking a different route to work might make you vulnerable to heavier traffic and being 5 minutes late, but it's not going to get you fired from your job. At home, play a board game and make your sole strategy to take risks whenever you can. So what if it backfires? It's only a game.

Inherent in all risks are feelings of anxiety and vulnerability. By giving yourself assignments to take small risks, you give yourself the chance to get used to uncomfortable feelings, in a safe manner.

Behavior therapists would call this an example of *systematic desensitization*—by taking small risks, you systematically desensitize yourself to the feeling of discomfort associated with risk and vulnerability.

As your comfort level increases, it becomes easier for you to deal with the discomfort of feeling vulnerable and thus solicit help when you need it.

Reach Out for Help

There is nothing wrong with the strategy of playing to one's strengths, but even so vulnerabilities still exist. A team can win with its powerful offense, but it is only a matter of time before its defensive vulnerability is exposed. While it's smart to develop your strengths, it's wise to identify and protect your vulnerabilities, as well.

We all have unique vulnerabilities in different areas of our lives. Some have vulnerability at work—a difficult personality style or a skill deficiency. Sometimes vulnerability is a family risk factor—college saving is impossible, not enough parenting time. Sometimes vulnerability is in marriage—not enough time together, poor communication skills, different goals. Whatever the vulnerability, it threatens the quality of your life.

You can identify specific vulnerabilities and strategies to deal with them—you can do that in discussions with your partner, family, and colleagues. But care soliciting works best when you acknowledge daily that because we live in an interactive world (the root of your cooperative instincts), there will naturally be many times when *you can help yourself by getting help from others*. Identifying these opportunities and taking advantage of your care soliciting instincts is using strategic evolutionary psychology.

It is essential that you actively are tuned to the strategy of getting others to aid and nurture you, whether it is help in building your business, taking care of your health, or keeping finances under control. "Look to get help," could be a care-soliciting slogan.

Who you ask for help is another issue.

7

The Importance of Ghost Busters

A common scenario is wanting to care solicit, but having no one to call on. Just as the blackbird chick can rely on its mother for aid, you, too, need to have people you can rely on to give you the nurturing and protection you need.

A lot of research indicates successful people have strong support systems. These support systems allow them to utilize their care-soliciting instincts. Many therapists have heard patients say numerous times that "Nothing is worse than going through a difficult situation by yourself." People who feel this way are often disconnected from this instinctual tool. Support systems not only serve as a means for protecting your weaknesses, but they also help you enhance your life. Some people call it having a "good network."

You need to have your own "ghost busters"—a support team—people you can call on. It is not easy to put together any good team, and your personal support team is no exception.

Building Your "A" Team

Mother Nature would recommend you select your team members on the basis of two criterions: trust and availability.

Who are the people you can really trust? Spend some time thinking about this. When your ancestors were faced with this task, natural selection favored those who made the right choice, because trust would allow each individual to rely on the other and act in a manner that would allow him to build long-term mutually beneficial relationships, which is usually the case in a trusting relationship.

For care soliciting, trust is foremost. You feel comfort in expressing your "weak" thoughts and feelings because you trust a person to respond caringly. When trust is high, you feel less at risk disclosing your problems, self-doubt, and neediness.

As you think about the people you trust, you become aware that you trust different people with different *vulnerability parts* of your life. For example, you may feel comfortable in discussing your intimate relationship—but not your financial woes—with a certain person. With someone else, it might be just the opposite. Areas of your life that you might need help with include work, health, marriage or an intimate relationship, finances, social life, parental relationships, and sibling relationships. Knowing in advance whom you can solicit care from in each arena when you are feeling vulnerable allows you to utilize your care-soliciting instincts quickly and get the help you need. You won't feel, "I'm all alone. There's nobody to help me."

After you deliberate about this, make a list of all the people who meet your trust criterion and next to their names list the areas of your life you would feel comfortable in asking for their help when needed.

Next, evaluate each person in respect to their *availability* to you. Availability is important because it increases your speed for getting support. Certainly, it was more beneficial to the clan to get the help it needed from within its group than having to travel overland to another clan. Today, you have a lot better chance of surviving a heart attack if there is a hospital within minutes, than if you have to drive an hour or wait an hour for an ambulance to arrive.

Thus, you may find that you are excluding people who are highly trustworthy. Parents who live in another state or a friend who's overwhelmed with her job and three kids, may be trustworthy, but if they're not available to you, they shouldn't make your list.

My suggestion would be to build a team that has at least four people so that there is always someone who can give you support. Do this by going down your list of trustworthy people and choose the first four that are most available to you. These four people make up your "A" team.

Using Your Team

Help comes in many ways. Sometimes, we get tangibles, such as a cash gift or loan. Other times, we get the care we need in the form of being listened to. Care comes in many packages.

How you use your support team is up to you, but my recommendation is to use them in at least three ways:

- To gain perspective
- To clarify your feelings
- To help you problem solve

Gain Perspective

Throughout life many incidents threaten our security. A possible job layoff, a project that overwhelms us, or a possible divorce are all examples that make most people feel extremely vulnerable. Yet most people confronted with these adversities fall into a thinking pattern that only makes the situation worse.

The majority of people seeking help through psychotherapy enter the therapy process with many "distorted thoughts." Indeed, these distorted thoughts intensify our feelings of vulnerability; we feel "extra" weak and overwhelmed. For example, an employee distorts a boss's critical comment into the thought, "My career is over," or a husband distorts the fact that his wife is 5 minutes late into, "The whole evening is ruined."

Distorted thinking, unique to humans, spurs the creation of *maladaptive cognitive adaptations*—like looking through a prism, distorted thoughts cause us to misperceive the reality of the situation, and these misperceptions often create moments of exaggerated feelings of vulnerability.

Other times, our thoughts are free from distortions, but nevertheless, we lock into a particular viewpoint that prevents us from moving forward. *Rigid thinking* is the semiclinical phrase.

Hundreds of studies in cognitive psychology and cognitive therapy confirm that your thinking directly influences your feelings. In the case of your distorted thoughts, which typically occur in stressful situations and encounters, these feelings are apt to be anxiety, anger, and fear, and they're very upsetting.

Instead of letting yourself be ruled by the reason of these distorted thoughts, call members of your "A" team and *solicit their care to help you gain perspective*. Gaining perspective on your situation allows you to deal with it much more effectively.

For a formula: Tell them what is happening. Tell them what you think. Ask them what they think. Reappraise the situation.

Bouncing Board

Unless you are an infant, it's hard to get help if you are a whiner. Instead of using your support team as a sounding board to vent your feelings, use them as a bouncing board to help you *clarify and validate your feelings*. When you call them, use another formula:

- Explain the situation.
- Ask them how they would feel in a similar situation. This helps you realize that you are not alone in your feelings and also the role, if any, of distorted thoughts.
- Think about your feelings after you have "bounced them around."

Sometimes, the care we need comes in the form of having someone just listen to our feelings. There have been many studies, for example, where results show that people just verbalizing their feelings to a tape recorder feel better afterward.

Telling a close friend you are distressed over the problems your daughter is experiencing in high school might not provide you with a brilliant new parenting tactic, but you will have your feelings listened to. This is just the type of care that can energize you to be helpful to your daughter. Similarly, sharing your frustration with a trusted coworker might not result in you developing a, "coping with your evil boss strategy," but you will still feel better for getting the feelings off your chest.

Problem Solving

We all have problems. It's the human condition. Those of us who are ineffective in dealing with them are apt to experience frustration, anger, and depression. With the latter, we frequently give up. Hello, depression.

If there is one thing that tells us we are vulnerable, it is when we have a dilemma we cannot solve ourselves. Instead of taking the road to depression, use your "A" team.

Whether it is in the form of helping you gain perspective, sorting out your feelings before you act, or helping you come up with a new response to an old problem, the care you receive places you in a much better position for dealing with the challenges that confront you. But you do have to solicit this nurturing.

Team Maintenance

You have put a lot of trust into your team, so you want to make sure you maintain it. The best way to do this is by demonstrating that support is mutual. In fact, the only way your team can survive is for you to support each of them in turn. Otherwise, they will start to feel that you are "a user," or selfish, and you run the risk of them not picking up when they see your name on their caller ID. Mutual support bonds your relationship, as it bonded the relationships of your ancestors; otherwise, clans would never have held together. Here are some everyday ways you can practice team maintenance:

- Ask each member what's going on in his life. This shows that you care, and their self-disclosing answers promote *intimacy*.
- Acknowledge the continuity of their lives by following through on past conversations—"How did that presentation go? "What did Everett say about your mother?" This shows that *you listened*.
- Demonstrate to your team how you *feel* about them, by talking about the positive feelings you have for them. This *nourishes* your relationship.

The more mutually supportive your relationships are, the easier you will find it to ask them for their time and wisdom.

Feeling comfortable with vulnerability, or at least acknowledging vulnerabilities, and having a support system are the prerequisites for using your care-soliciting instincts. With these in place, it is easier for you to evoke your "nurture me" instinct, and you then have another evolutionary tool of success at your disposal.

8

Care Soliciting Today

How often do you care solicit to protect yourself? "Rarely," I bet is your answer.

Because those people who can practice their evolutionary tools in a wide variety of ways and in multiple contexts are going to be the most successful, it's best for you to evoke your care soliciting broadly—in the context of yourself, your partner, your family, and your profession.

I'll help you get the knack of care soliciting by providing some examples and applications of when and how to care solicit in some common scenarios. You will see that in each case, despite that asking for help increases the chances for success, we seldom do it, even when *how* we would care solicit and *who* we would call is obvious.

Care Soliciting Helps Take the Weight Off

Numerous studies show that the majority of us have health vulnerabilities. What are yours? Right off the bat, if you are an average American, you are plump, and your health is at risk. Millions of Americans are literally eating years off their lives by obesity.

Consider how most of us attempt to address this vulnerability, and fail. I'd bet that you know at least two dozen people in the last year or two who have taken the traditional routes—following diets, going to support groups, or going cross country to a weight rehab resort. The best scenario usually results in a weight change, sudden change of habits, but a few months later, the pounds are back.

Note that in the traditional routes, the individual is making a *solo* effort. Even in the case of support groups, the individual must be able to self-motivate to take advantage of the group. Yet, more often than not, the individual is unable to maintain the regimen, skips meetings, and slides back into the bad habits that made them fat. As to following a diet, the intention might be there, but it is another thing to do the cooking and shopping for your meals, let alone have the discipline to stick to it. These solo efforts rarely work, and if you are one of the plump, you know this to be true. Care soliciting might yield different results.

In this case, you would care solicit from either your partner or a member of your support team to help you eat healthier and exercise daily. Most importantly, you would have to express to them that *you are incapable of doing this by yourself*—you have tried numerous times to no avail. Tell them you need their help and *how* they can help you. In the case of your partner, it might be that for the next month or two, he or she takes responsibility for shopping for the foods you can eat and maybe even prepare them for you—*it won't happen if you rely on yourself*. Or you might ask a team member to start an exercise class with you—you've started many in the past but quickly drop out. The buddy system could be the support you need to achieve success, and the time spent together strengthens your friendship.

What makes care soliciting difficult here is that you have to acknowledge your weakness—you do not have the ability to do this by yourself, and you fear that you might be refused the help you need. However, by acknowledging this weakness, and assuming you have a strong and mutually supportive relationship with your partner or team member, there is a good chance that your 911 call will be answered.

Not having to do it by yourself takes the some of the burden off yourself and a lot of that extra weight off yourself, too.

House Cleaning Bills

The physical differences (not social learning or cultural norms) between early man and woman led to gender-assigned roles in their culture. Since males are stronger than females, it would have made little sense for your female ancestors to hunt the giant bears, since their lesser physical strength would handicap them. Better they stay at home while the stronger males go on the week-long hunts. Each sex had to play its role for the clan to thrive. The end result of this is that both sexes have become hardwired to think of themselves in gender-specific work roles. Males are hardwired to think of themselves as the provider and protector, while females are hardwired to think that their job is to take care of the kids and the home.

Even in today's world, we see the persistence of our *hardwiring roles*. Men still seem to think of themselves as providers, and women still tend to think of themselves as homemakers. Indeed, many women feel guilty when they are career-oriented instead of marriage/family-oriented—on the "mommy track." The evolutionary interpretation would be that the guilt stems from going against their hardwiring, against their nature. And many men experience discomfort playing house dad, because of their hardwired instincts.

Many times, these hardwiring roles with their associated sets of beliefs are *cognitive maladaptions* and make it difficult for people to care solicit from their mate, when in fact, that is exactly what is needed. Two common examples come to mind. One of the biggest sources of conflict in a marriage is finances. In coaching, counseling sessions, and dozens of workshops, I've had both presidents of companies and blue collar workers alike complain to me that their family finances are out of control.

When I ask members from either group how they handle their home budget problems, I note two consistent points that come into play. The first to surface is that even when both parents have careers, males still take "ownership" of the financial welfare of the family. The second point is I always hear the same "solutions"—from trying to instill a family budget to explaining finances in detail to cutting back on "extras." More often than not, members from both high and lower incomes report that such efforts fail, and conversations about the issues usually end in arguments. Perhaps your own experiences are similar.

Care soliciting offers a different solution for this contemporary problem but is rarely used because of the hardwiring provider and protector male belief, which today, is a cognitive maladaption. This belief inhibits care soliciting; to do so would imply failing at their role. It's a message we've seen thousands of times in movies and television: "What kind of husband are you? You can't support us," represents some of the poorer dialogue.

The story continues that in his effort to be the provider, and not wanting to appear and feel weak and vulnerable, the husband keeps the climbing debt to himself, increasing financial vulnerability and generating much more stress and conflict in the marriage. These are very good predictors for divorce.

If only care soliciting had been applied. Instead of trying to dictate a financial plan to follow, or complain to your spouse, or announce a series of cutbacks, care soliciting here would take the form of sitting down with your partner and sharing your feelings of vulnerability about the family's financial condition. Expressing your feelings of anxiety and the beliefs and *facts* they are based on—not being able to afford college, not being able to pay the mortgage as rates get reset—is crucial to the conversation. Then, you care solicit by telling your partner that you need their help in responding to your financial situation. How they can best give that help is up to them but, you need their help.

A president of a company told me that when he said this to his wife, she cut down her jewelry buying. A construction worker told me his wife started buying in bulk and making economical dinners from scratch without sacrificing the tastiness or nutrition of the meals.

Similarly, I have heard many wives and mothers complain that the relentless workload of running a household is brutal. But because their hardwiring belief tells them they should be adept at managing the household/cave, they become reticent to say otherwise. For some reason, they prefer to become depressed, obese, a victim of migraine headaches, and a shrew to their mate.

Care soliciting here would be Mother Nature's advice: Ask your partner for help. The arena could be your kitchen or your living room, but you must sit down and express your vulnerability: You are feeling overwhelmed with running the household. Rather than complaining, the female here informs her partner about her daily tasks and shares that it is hard for her to do it by herself, despite her desire. "I need some help from you," she says. "Maybe you could pick up the dry cleaning on your way home from work, or drop the kids off at school in the morning, or fix dinner every Wednesday. I just feel I can't do it all by myself. I need your help."

Care soliciting in both these examples teaches us a valuable lesson: Making yourself vulnerable to your mate can help you get your financial house in order and keep it clean at the same time.

Care Soliciting at Work

A perfect time to take advantage of your care-soliciting instincts is at the end of a performance appraisal.

Performance appraisal is a term familiar to almost the entire working world. In theory, both parties share their evaluations of the subordinate's performance, with the mutual goal of improving performance in the year to come. After a productive dialogue, there is an agreed-upon action plan listing the steps to take that will lead to improvement. Unfortunately, the steps prescribed usually lead to little or no improvement.

I've found that the problem here lies not in the steps recommended or the motivation of the employee. Rather, all too often the individual lacks the knowledge or skills for implementation. The post-appraisal employees don't improve because they don't know how to improve, or they know how but can't do it on their own.

It's ironic to me, for example, that the sales rep is asked to improve her sales when she is having trouble in sales to begin with. Similarly, it doesn't make sense to tell a D student to do better if he is doing his best. The missing link in a performance appraisal for many employees is that there is no one to help them. This is where care soliciting comes into play.

I have asked hundreds of managers who have given performance appraisals and hundreds of individuals who have been appraised. I know that specifically asking for help is rare. Sometimes help is offered, but it is rarely requested by the individual being appraised.

Applied to a performance appraisal, the individual can care solicit by saying: "I am looking forward to improving, but to do so I need some help. Can you help me? Maybe you can be my coach. Or maybe you can tell me someone else I can approach for help, but I do know that I need help to improve."

There are other ways to care solicit at work, too. Many organizations have mentoring programs, but in the typical company, you are *assigned* a mentor, usually after you have reached some occupational level of success. Care soliciting as it is described here would dictate that you *request* a mentor to help you when you feel you need it, not when your organization merits you worthy of having one. Organizations lose a lot of employee diamonds-in-the-rough because they do not encourage their folks to ask for mentors.

Sometimes, the best way to care solicit at work is to identify who can best help you (caregiver) and literally plead for the person's aid, like the young resident who was doing subpar in his surgical rotation. He approached his surgical professor and said, "Sir, I am not going to do well in my surgical rotation if you don't help me. Please, help me be successful. It is a matter of life and death."

Building Your Business

Consultants, attorneys, therapists, dentists, tutors, financial advisors, insurance agents, real estate agents, physicians, and accountants are only some of the entrepreneurial professions. A common denominator for all of them is that it's tough to build clientele. Mother Nature would instruct all these people to make it easier for themselves by care soliciting for business.

Yet, few people take advantage of care soliciting to build their business, the probable reason being the widely held belief that if you ask for business, you will be perceived in the eyes of those you ask as weak, someone who needs the business. For the financial advisor, this plays out along these lines, "If I ask my client for a referral, she will think I need the business; that my business is faltering because I'm not good at it. She will conclude that I must be a poor financial advisor." The only truth in this line of thinking is that by not asking for business, the financial advisor will be a *poor* financial advisor.

The truth is, professionals solicit for business every day. Some people do it in the form of advertising; a law firm's commercial on TV is care soliciting your business, as is that of the computer company and the sandwich shop. They are all asking you to help build their business by buying their products and services. And those who can attract your business most effectively are the ones who thrive.

How do you contemporize your care-soliciting instincts to build your own business?

Answering three questions will help you:

- Who can throw you business?
- When is the time to care solicit?
- How will you do it?

How you answer these questions, of course, depends on how you make a living. I'll illustrate their application in the case of a financial advisor, and then you can think about how you would do it for yourself.

I'm the financial advisor. First, I decide who can refer new clients to me. I know from what my branch manager tells me and from my research on the industry that the best source for referrals is my existing clients. But I know that every client is not a referral source. It has to be those who I have already helped, made an impact in their lives. These clients have confidence in me, they trust me, and this makes it easier for them to be confident in referring their colleagues, friends, and relatives to me. I make a list of my top referral client sources.

Now, I have to think about *when* is the best time to care solicit. I can't imagine myself calling a client like, say, Bill Smith, and flat-out asking for referrals. I will have to do it in the right context. For me, it is when I am having a face-to-face conversation with my client, one in which I am giving him good news about the growth of his portfolio. I know my moment to care solicit has arrived when the client says something along the lines of, "Hey, this is really good news. You are doing a terrific job with my investments." As I hear my client thank me, I conclude that he sees value in my work, likes me, and is in a good mood. There is no better time for me to care solicit. Soliciting now becomes less risky. It is just a question of how to do it.

I have my own repertoire of referral-soliciting techniques, but in this case, when my client is thanking me, my phrasing sounds like this: "I m happy that you are pleased. Let me know if you have some friends or family members who I can help, too." Or I might put it like this: "I would certainly appreciate the opportunity of providing the same service to some of your friends." And I even might even say, "Feel free to recommend my services."

I am well aware that my efforts might not be successful all the time, but whenever they are, I am ahead of the game. Inevitably, I know that care soliciting from my clients will pay off. When I focus on the who, when, and how, I increase my chances for getting the help I need, and this feeling makes it more comfortable for me to ask.

Think of how you can solicit for business. A group of physicians with a top-notch practice in my hometown do it with plaques that are visible throughout their offices. They read: "The greatest compliment you can give us is to let us care for your loved ones." This is care soliciting at its cleverest.

The Care-Soliciting President

A CEO of a major company was fired. According to insiders, the CEO could be described as being very independent. He dismissed and stiffed the input from others and was seen as arrogant: "I'm the boss." Also, according to the same reliable sources, in board meetings, he greatly minimized the fourth-quarter loss that the company would soon suffer. The final nail in the coffin was that, unbeknown to the board of directors, he had made inquiries about merging with another company. These last two points particularly peeved the board, and a career ended with a no-confidence ousting.

This story was big news in the financial pages, but I've heard it numerous times. A president or CEO of a company (of any size) develops vulnerability—perhaps major investments are "going south." He minimizes or distorts the reality of the situation until, inevitably, the problems are exposed.

Over and over, I have noticed the tendency for the top person to promote the message that, "We are doing fantastic," when in reality, the bottom line proves otherwise. These leaders doom themselves because they let their vulnerabilities go unprotected. They don't acknowledge the problem so that it can be swiftly addressed. Worse, because they keep it to themselves, they end up acting maladaptive, like the aforementioned CEO who approached another company on the sly.

Mother Nature would have advised this CEO: "The best way to cover your back is to care solicit. Go to your board and your department heads and level with them. Tell them the company is vulnerable, and you need their help to protect it. Your forthrightness and integrity will be respected. And, while you still may be out of a job, at least you can increase the odds that you can protect the welfare of your company, which is what you were hired to do."

Presidents would be wise to connect with their care-soliciting instincts. A beginning would be to forget the "It's our best year ever speech," and substitute an accurate State of the Union message that addresses the organization's vulnerabilities. Honesty enables you to rally your troops to take swift corrective maneuvers.

Similarly, managers would be smart to hold *vulnerability meetings* where the purpose is to find out what is going wrong. The earlier these points surface, the faster protection can start.

Leaders in charge at all levels need to communicate to those they lead that "It's okay to ask for help, and those who do will get help." This helps create a care-soliciting culture, and it pays off in morale, staff retention, and profits.

There Will Always Be Kryptonite

It's simple: Care soliciting will always be important because you, and all future humans, will always have vulnerabilities to protect. Often, it is not possible to do it by yourself. I remember a Superman episode in which he is lying on the floor, weakened by the one thing that made him vulnerable—Kryptonite. Despite the fact it was only a few feet from where he lay, he was too weak to crawl away. Just when it appeared he was a goner, Lois Lane and Jimmy Olson ran into the room, threw the Kryptonite into a lead barrel, and Superman's strength returned.

There will always be Kryptonite in your life, but if you allow yourself to care solicit, you will also find that there are plenty of Lois Lanes and Jimmy Olsons.

Why Care Soliciting Works

Mother Nature would tell you to be confident that your care-soliciting efforts will be rewarded. The reason for her confidence is that she has created a fail-safe system. She has hardwired into those you care solicit a reciprocal tool for enhancing your life—*care giving*. Thus, *your care-soliciting instincts work because they stimulate care-giving instincts in others.* Care giving is your next instinctual tool for life enhancement.

Part III

Care Give...So You Can Develop the Future

Enhance your life by using your care giving instincts

9

Developing the Future

Your Evolutionary Heritage

*A wolf stands over a frozen bird and begins eating it while his lit-
ter mate watches hungrily. Then, when he has eaten more than half
the bird, he rises, carries the carcass and lays it a foot from his sister's
nose. He then waits beside it as she delicately takes it. Later in the
week, the same wolf carries a fresh-killed hare in his mouth for more
than two miles to feed his sick brother.*

Care-giving behavior comes in many forms, like the preceding
illustrations of bonds of allegiance. It includes nurturing, providing
safety and security, and being responsive to the needs of others, especially the young. Its function as an evolutionary tool is that providing
care to others, especially the young, boosts the odds that the organizational unit will continue to flourish. Care giving, then, is nature's
inherent tool for developing others, or more broadly, for advancing
the future. For this reason, Mother Nature has made sure you are a
caregiver.

Designer Genes

Human babies, like animal newborns, are born helpless, needing
to be entirely cared for and protected. Fortunately, they are born with

all the necessary tools and "instructions" (care-soliciting instincts) to attain such care for themselves and to become a loved and loving part of their family and society.

The ingrained neural and hormonal interactions between parent and child are among the most powerful in nature. The hormonal cues are clear and compelling, and our instincts provide us with all the appropriate responses. Parents naturally follow the signals of their neurons and hormones, nurturing their babies and maintaining physical closeness with them. Just as your genes are designed to solicit care, so are they designed to give care.

To this point, a cuckoo does an interesting thing with its eggs. When she's ready to lay an egg, the mother cuckoo doesn't build its own nest, but instead lays her egg in another bird's nest. The bird sets on the egg, and when the baby cuckoo hatches, she nurtures it as if it were her own. Either the foster mother is unable to recognize the alien cuckoo as an intruder or the chick's cries for food are so potent a stimulus she doesn't care.

Like the cuckoo, you too are hardwired with the nurturing drive. This is why parents who cannot have children often adopt or become foster parents. Mother Nature would say it provides them the opportunity to express their care-giving instincts. We are not only hardwired to become caregivers, but we are also hardwired to express our care-giving instincts.

Mother Nature's Chemistry Course: Female

Oxytocin is a chemical messenger released in the brain chiefly in response to social contact and is especially pronounced with skin-to-skin contact. The hormonal-like substance promotes bonding patterns and creates desire for further contact with the infant or adult who sparks these spikes in oxytocin.

Oxytocin is one of nature's chief tools for creating a mother. Stimulated by the high levels of estrogen (female hormone) during pregnancy, the number of oxytocin receptors in the expectant mother's brain multiplies dramatically near the end of her pregnancy. These receptors increase in the part of her brain that promotes maternal behavior.

After birth, a mother continues to produce elevated levels of oxytocin as a consequence of nursing and holding her infant, and the levels are based on the amount of such contact. The hormonal condition provides a sense of calm and well-being.

High oxytocin causes a mother to become familiar with the unique odor of her newborn infant and prefer her own baby's odor above all others. Baby is similarly imprinted on mother, deriving feelings of calmness and pain reduction along with mom. When the infant is born, he is already imprinted on the odor of his *amniotic fluid.* This odor imprint helps him find (care solicit) mother's nipple, which has a similar odor. In the days following birth, the infant is comforted by the odor of the milk.

Under the early influence of oxytocin, nerve junctions in certain areas of the mother's brain actually undergo reorganization, thereby making her maternal behaviors hardwired.

Mother Nature's Chemistry Course: Male

You don't have to be a fashion conscious male to wear designer "genes." *Vasopressin* is a hormone that promotes (hardwires) brain reorganization toward paternal behaviors while the male is cohabitating with the pregnant mother. Stimulated by nearness and touch, vasopressin promotes bonding between the father and the mother, helps the father recognize and bond to his baby, and makes him want to be part of the family, rather than alone. The father becomes more dedicated to his mate and more protective, just like the male prairie vole.

Vasopressin reinforces the father's testosterone protective inclination, but tempers his aggression, making him more reasonable and less extreme. By promoting more rational and less capricious thinking, this hormone induces a sensible paternal role, providing stability as well as vigilance.

Thus, regardless of your sex, Mother Nature has hardwired you to be a caregiver. If she hadn't, parents would not *feel compelled* to nurture their young, leading to infant mortality and quick extinction. From an evolutionary perspective, both sexes are hardwired to nurture and protect because it enhances life for the individual, family, community, and, of course, the world.

10

I Gave at the Office

Care giving is perceived as a positive attribute in people, so it is not surprising that most people *overestimate* how often and how well they care give. We all give care in different ways and at different times, so it might be enlightening for you to think about the times and reasons you minimize and become disconnected from your care-giving tools. Maybe they are similar to the ones I have heard and observed in my clinical, coaching, teaching, and consulting experiences.

The Anger Excuse

In therapy sessions, I hear the "anger excuse" time and time again: "I was angry, so I didn't want to show care." When mismanaged, anger permeates a relationship; it extinguishes the nurturing instinct. Because most people are not adept at anger management, you can begin to see why so many people in so many relationships accuse their partner of not caring.

Anger, like all emotions, has a survival function. At the dawn of man, it served as a protective mechanism by mobilizing your physical resources so that men and women could *feel* confident about confronting the "wrongness" of the situation.

However, in the course of evolving human relationships, anger too has evolved its functions. One that is relevant here is that anger is often used to combat the feelings of being psychologically wounded, *feeling hurt.* Also, anger toward another person often results in *withholding behavior*, a modern expression of anger-aggression: Instead of attacking someone, we freeze them out.

Your partner, for example, is flirty at a party and ignores you. You become angry, but you keep it inside. A day or two later, you recognize that your spouse is feeling down and needs a hug. But you turn away because you are still angry—anger has inhibited your affection instinct.

You already know that your human nature is to avoid feeling vulnerable so, instead of feeling wounded, you get infuriated. The longer you stay angry at your partner, the longer you ignore her needs and distance yourself.

This can occur often in the course of a relationship. Psychological hurt is experienced, but instead of dealing with feelings of vulnerability, anger becomes the relationship response, and affection and communication become relationship-rare, and the bond unravels.

You can keep your bond vibrant by dealing with the hurtful behavior openly and immediately. Say: "I feel hurt" instead of "I feel angry." The former can be healed; the latter keeps bad blood flowing.

No Time to Give

If you don't spend time with someone, it is pretty hard to demonstrate and communicate affection, whether it is with your partner, kids, employees, or your parents. Indeed, many people lose contact with their care-giving instincts because they do not spend time with the people who would benefit from their love and attention.

Mother Nature recognizes this need. It's why there are particular lengths of time that a baby is dependent on the mother—to ensure the mother spends the necessary amount of time to protect and nurture her child.

How much time you spend with your family, clients, and employees gives you an idea if a lack of time with these people is why you're out of touch with your nurturing instinct.

It's Too Much Effort

From your earliest moments of being a caregiver, you quickly learn it is hard, draining, and sometimes even painful. Many people just do not want to demonstrate their nurturing instinct because it is too much of an effort.

Take the common contemporary example of demonstrating care to a loved one—giving a birthday present. Or letting a friend know you empathize with his adversity or joy by sending a Hallmark card or making a phone call. I surveyed many people as to why they do not engage in these simple acts, and, believe it or not, the number one reason was, "It's too much of an effort."

It does take an effort to drive an hour to visit your father in a nursing home. It takes an effort to taxi your kids back and forth to soccer games and dance recitals, and spend the evening after dinner helping your daughter research her history report, especially when you're drained from work and commuting. Care giving takes energy and sometimes, you just don't have it to give.

I'll Help You Lose

Our competitive instinct, too, can trump our nurturing instinct. This is particularly true in the working environment where, for many people, competition with their colleagues dominates their working attitude.

Because competition typically is a win/lose scenario, many people are reluctant to help others win because it makes themselves "lose" in comparison. "Why should I help her get ahead of me?" To do so would stir up painful feelings of inferiority. In effect, by not helping your coworker, you help him "lose."

To some extent, this line of thinking is hardwired—your instinct to survive. The sales reps who compete for bonuses with their colleagues tend to keep "success" tips for closing the deal to themselves. If they develop their colleagues, they might end up literally losing their jobs. Disconnecting from care giving here helps such reps to not only boost their professional status, but also to maintain a *feeling* of superiority. Later, we see how Mother Nature helps us harness our competitive drive to actually encourage care giving/development rather than inhibit it.

It Is Expensive

Nurturing in all its forms can be a risky endeavor. It costs a lot of money to give your parents the best care; your children the best "developmental" opportunities, such as tutors, or dance, music, and karate lessons; or your pet the high-end food and frequent veterinarian care.

Obviously, few of us have unlimited resources of time or money. As a result, even when we want to do "everything we can to help," such as visiting a hospitalized relative or friend, the airfare makes the intention prohibitive. The same would be true for the country that wants to help impoverished countries all over the world—the desire is there, but the resources are not. Lack of resources, especially finances and time, is a frequent and realistic reason that prevents people from exhibiting certain care-giving behaviors and communications. This, along with mismanaged emotions, lack of time and energy, and our competitive drive are all undercurrents that pull us away from our natural urge to actualize our care-giving instincts and, thus, prevent us from enhancing our lives to their fullest.

11 —————————————

Care Giving Today

You can begin to cultivate your nurturing instinct with the knowledge that care giving is evolutionarily defined as a *collection of behaviors and communications* that attend to the needs of others for *the purpose of developing* the other. We nurture others so that we can ensure the future. And, too, maximizing the genius of your caregiving instincts nourishes your own life. Here are a few examples of how you can use this evolutionary tool to develop and secure your ecological niche in your most important life arenas.

Some of Mother Nature's Parenting Advice

I can't think of a better expert on parenting than Mother Nature. She's been doing it longer than anyone, and she's raised all sorts of kids. If you asked her for advice on care-giving principles for your kids, here's what she would say.

Prioritize Your Children

Back on the Savannah, parents who made it a priority to keep their offspring clean and well-fed experienced lower infant mortality, and their children were sure to grow up healthier to perpetuate their family tree.

The same is true today. Parents who make their children a priority reap the benefits of having children who have more enhanced lives. Do you make care giving to your kids a priority? Only you know for sure. If your three-year-old daughter has a bad cold, do you stay home from work or drop her off at daycare? Do you give up a business meeting or a round of golf with a client to sit in the front row at your son's school play, or do you tell him, "I wish I could have been there but I had to work." Is it more important for you to watch the playoffs on TV or take your kids for a picnic at the park? Do you buy that status car or save the money for a summer camp experience or a teen tour?

Please understand that there are no "correct" answers, only answers that help you increase your awareness of whether you actually make care giving to your children your first priority. Those people who do reap the rewards.

Provide a Safe and Secure Environment

Most people think that providing a safe and secure environment for children is easy and the norm. But consider how many household accidents there are due to parental carelessness, such as not baby-proofing the home, or the number of children who are abused and molested by a parent while the other parent turns a blind eye and fails to protect the children. Add in all the kids whose health care and dental needs are neglected, and it seems that parents who provide a safe and secure environment for their children might be a smaller population than we may think.

What about you? Do you make sure your child is in a physically safe environment at school? Are you a super-sleuth when it comes to investigating babysitters? Do you protect your child from being treated unfairly or harshly by teachers or other children? Do you make it safe for your kids to express their thoughts and feelings? Honest answers tell you how well you honor your nurturing obligations.

Spend a Lot of Time with Your Kids

In the course of a week, how much time do you actually spend with your kids? Our ancestors, who spent virtually every hour of their lives with their children, had sturdy emotional bonds, thus ensuring family cohesiveness and the likelihood that aging parents would be able to rely on their children, in turn.

We often speak about the importance of quality time with our kids, but quantity of time is equally important. That a pregnancy is nine months long is one of Mother Nature's mechanisms for getting the mother to spend time with the newborn-to-be. During this time literally spent as one, mother and baby are already bonding.

When your children start school, develop friendships, and, later, set their own agendas, time spent together lessens. That's why spending *lots of time with your children in their early years is highly recommended.* From infancy to age two is a critical time during which parents and child become attuned to the emotional cues between each other that later go on to enhance their relationship. If you missed this opportunity and your kids are older, you might consider blocking out set periods of time that you will just be with your kids.

Do Interactive Activities

It's one thing to watch your son play in a tennis match, but Mother Nature would tell you it's much better to *play* tennis *with* him. The early parents who interacted frequently with their kids and included them in activities such as food gathering, hunting, and gardening taught them the skills and values that would give their kids the survival edge.

Think of the types of activities you do with your children and make them as interactive as possible. If you read a story to your daughter, ask her to tell you a story, too. There is nothing wrong with watching television with your son on a Saturday afternoon, but turn it into an interactive learning activity by discussing the show, the feelings it arouses, and how characters handled specific situations. For years, I watched my daughter's favorite television shows with her because it provided a forum to discuss issues that were important to her and provided me with examples of what she liked that could be used to teach her valuable skills, such as problem solving: "What would you do if you were in that situation?" Of course, I could only speak during the commercials.

Educate Your Children

Care giving is about developing, and parents who learned that education was essential to their child's development were thinking the same way that good parents do today.

Education has always been important because it allows an individual to achieve mobility, to move through his environment to secure a valuable niche. Without education, the individual stays stuck and increases the likelihood of failing—in evolutionary terms—to become extinct.

Parents who educate their children well prepare them to cope with and alter their life course. "I want a better life for my children," is the way it is often expressed. Knowing this is a fundamental instinct, it's a sad commentary that so many young people in America drop out of school without learning basic reading and writing skills. Do you think the parents of these children follow Mother Nature's advice?

Do you actively participate in your children's education? Do you go to school meetings, schedule teacher conferences, help with homework, and do everything possible to ensure that your child is getting and succeeding in an excellent education?

University tuition and costs are already staggering and are sure to continue spiraling upward. Are you saving and investing money now for your children's tuition, or are you planning to burden them with student loans? A strong recommendation from Mother Nature: Squirrel away as much money as you can for your child's education.

Love Me Tending, Love Me Sweet

The early man who tended to the needs of his woman increased the likelihood that she would care for him, in turn, as well as provide a loving and secure environment for their children. Similarly, the early woman who tended to the needs of her bedmate was more likely to keep him providing for her and their children, and I'm sure it doesn't surprise you that when partners nurture each other, both experiences positive results. *Tending*, a term often used for care giving in marriage, is a life enhancer for the entire family.

In marriages where tending is absent, divorce is inevitable. Single people get sick more and for longer periods than married people. They make more visits to physicians, and they are more vulnerable to infectious diseases, especially fatal ones. It gets worse in that they become especially vulnerable to depression and are way more likely to seek psychiatric help than people who remain married and receive tending benefits. The opposite is true for individuals in relationships where tending to each other is high.

How might you best tend to your own partner and marriage? Here are two evolutionary guided recommendations. The first: Tend to your partner's *physical health*. In the early millennia, women who ensured that their mates were well rested, fed fresh food, and who freed them from the stresses of having to deal with household responsibilities and troubles were more likely to keep their mates healthier so that they could be good providers. It's not surprising that today married men are healthier and make more money than single men. For women, tending to her partner's health enhanced her own life.

How tuned in are you to your partner's health? Do you know when your partner is due for crucial check-ups and do you urge him to have them? Do you encourage and help him to eat healthy and exercise daily? When your partner is tired, do you tell her to relax while you take care of her needs? Mother Nature proudly says that women do this much better than men, so men should take note here: Tend to your wife's health needs, and it will make your own life richer.

The second recommendation: Tend to your partner's *mental health* in an area *she* finds stressful. For example, women's health is damaged severely by marital conflict and conflict with friends and family members. This is understandable when you consider that many of the responsibilities women had to succeed in, such as child rearing and food gathering, depended on their ability to forge relationships with other women. Conflict in these relationships posed a threat to a woman succeeding in these tasks, and thus by extension, a threat to her keeping her partner. It was antisurvival and distressing.

Men who want to be more tending are continually tuned in to the "news" of their partner's relationships, especially to conflict that might be happening with her friends, family, and children. When she appears to be distressed over these relationships or wants to vent about them, the tending male listens, perhaps helps her problem solve, and does both sweetly.

In contrast, men find career events and work relationships to be their own major source of distress. It shouldn't be surprising when you remember that the hardwired role of provider still plays out today. A bad hunt or conflict with the chieftain was sure to be as stressful as today's bad day at the office and tiff with the boss. A tending female now needs to be supportive and encouraging to her partner's work efforts. Let him know you are tuned in to the economic realities of the world, and do it sweetly, too.

Many studies bear out this gender difference. Women manifest more adverse physiological reactions when speaking about marital conflict and family relationship problems. Men, in the same studies, show little detrimental response when these subjects are discussed but do show adverse physiological responses when they speak of problems and conflict at work. Blame Mother Nature for this.

It is clear that partners who tend to each other reap individual and mutual benefits. Their tending behaviors and communications develop their marriage and ensure they will have a longer life span and healthier and happier lives, more of the "better" than the "worse."

The Care Bear Boss

In hunting parties and other community tasks, clan leaders saw that some members needed more help than others learning the skills and working together. Rather than ignore them and let them fall behind, the leaders were patient in teaching them, so they could go on to be successful and "pull their weight." In return, they became grateful and loyal to their caring boss. Even if given the opportunity to join another clan, they didn't. Their bonds of allegiance were to their caring leader.

It's okay to be a gruff bear at work as long as you remember that part of your evolutionary heritage is that you are a "Care bear," too. It is well known in both the academic and business world that managers who are attentive and caring toward their team reap many benefits: better relationships, a motivated and productive staff, retention of talented employees, strong bottom line, and greater career success.

How do you demonstrate care to your staff? Many do it by thoughtful gestures such as sending employees a birthday card or taking the gang out to lunch. More significant than these goodwill gestures is giving your team recognition for ideas, innovation, and a standard of excellence.

Development is key: training, mentoring, and constructive evaluation. Take time to reflect on the specifics of how well you train and develop your staff. Do you send them to classes and seminars? And, do you make sure the training you provide is effective? It's been my experience that training is too often evaluated superficially. All organizations would spend their training dollar smarter if they increased their rigor in evaluating its actual benefit to their staff.

Moreover, organizations should ascertain whether the training they provide to their employees is *meaningful*—does it actually enhance their lives? Training in the basic tasks of a job is essential, but training that captures and demonstrates your care giving is *employee meaningful training*—it contributes to the development and enhancement of the employees' overall lives. Training on a new software program, or how to do an inventory, might be essential to their tasks, but I know from years of experience that a manager's employees find a training class on giving and taking criticism, emotional intelligence, and life balance to be deeply meaningful in their lives and improve team building and job performance, as well.

Make it a priority to ask each of your direct reports what they specifically need (emotional nutrients) to feel they are developing themselves, and then follow up and do your best to provide it to them. The evolutionary tip here is to provide training to your staff that communicates you know what their challenges are and that you want to help them.

Care bear bosses also take issue with the corporate conventional wisdom of keeping personal problems out of the workplace. It's easy to see why. As a clan community evolved, its members assumed specialized work roles. However, unlike today, everyone at work also lived together. While they worked together, the conversation would turn to other aspects of their community, topics ranging from child care to fights with their woman. Sharing these personal issues and how they could be handled became a way in which "workers" could give care and support to each other. In this sense, bringing personal issues to work is hardwired into us because our ancestors found it was a way to get help.

Today, it is uncommon for an entire staff to actually live together—outside of an oil rig or a kibbutz—but we still have the same personal issues that our ancestors had, and talking about them at work should not be universally frowned-upon.

Care bear bosses *make the time* to help their staff deal with personal issues. This attention can be simply listening to the problems they are having with their children, or the pain of their divorce. Other times, it is demonstrated by granting time off to fulfill family obligations. And naturally, Care bear bosses are rewarded with greater performance and retention of key talent. "Care today, they are here tomorrow," could be a Care bear boss slogan.

Care Giving to Elders

One of the ways knowledge is gained is through the process of *generational transmission*—an older generation passes down crucial information to the next generation. For example, creatures know their enemies at first glance because previous generations have hardwired it into their DNA. An infant who cries when she sees a stranger for the first time is acting on a hardwired instinct from its ancestral mother: "Beware of strangers."

At the dawn of man, life span was short, so you can see that passing on information was a challenge for our ancestors. As a result, it would often be the case that the community could not fully maximize the learning and wisdom the elders had amassed from their life experiences, thus clan development stalled. In effect, each generation had to reinvent the wheel. If enough of a senior generation died before it could teach the community skills and cultural values, the community would inevitably become extinct. This also occurred in clans that paid little attention to their elders.

On the other hand, there were communities that realized the longer they kept their elders healthy, the longer the community was able to take advantage of their knowledge, a vital commodity that helped any tribe flourish. Thus, it came to pass that ensuring that the elders remained healthy evolved into a primal instinct. Care giving to the elderly became a means, an adaptation, for investing in the young. Countless generations found this to be true, so it is no wonder that somebody inevitably captured Mother Nature's recommendation: "Respect your elders!" That is both an instinctual urge and a value hardwired into cultures.

Nurturing and protecting the elderly takes many forms. In organizations, care giving is implemented through executive *development* programs. These are the programs that companies run internally or in conjunction with a business school. The focus is to help the senior executives develop new skills, conceptual and behavioral, that enhance their effectiveness. Organizations that are rich in executive development programs communicate the message to their senior staff that they have much to contribute; they are on their way up, not down. In fact, I've had many executives who attend these programs tell me, "I feel good about being here, because it tells me my company cares about me." Mother Nature would instruct people in human resources, training, and development to assess "How do we develop our *senior* people so they can contribute more to our younger employees?" In the financial service industry, senior advisors are valued not just for their productivity but for what they pass on to younger generations, which is why they are asked to give presentations to the young men and women fresh out of business school.

What about care giving to your own parents? Here it comes in the form of giving comfort, physical assistance, financial help, and other nutrients that enhance their sunset years. If great distance separates you, you can show your care through phone calls, letters, and emails.

There are other ways to demonstrate care to your parents, too. Do they need help taking care of their bills, their homes, or shopping? If so, help them! If you can't, do some research to find out who can. Perhaps there are many organizations in their neighborhood that offer care to the elderly, be it a phone call every morning to check on their welfare, a home visit to clean and prepare meals, or a shuttle service to take them to the senior center, the library, and the market. One friend pays a taxi company by the month to drive her grandmother around her small town. She says she's become the most popular "old lady" in town because she'll pick up her friends and get them out of the house, too. Your instinctual duty is to make your aging parents' lives easier so that they can live independently as long as they can, because for many years when you were young that was their job. Lion kings know this is part of the circle of life.

I've known many people who find it extremely stressful to be a full-time caregiver to their aging parents, especially when they're ill or compromised by Alzheimer's disease. Remember to take *respite*. Just as a mother needs a break from care giving to her children, you, too, need a break from care giving to your parents. Respite allows you to recharge.

It should not be surprising that despite the stresses associated with providing care to elderly parents, children continue to do it. It is more than an act of love. Mother Nature would tell us we do it to because we are hardwired to feel that nurturing our parents is a responsibility, and by continuing this responsibility, we increase the chance that our children will take care of us, in turn.

This value is hardwired. It explains why so many people feel guilty when they neglect their aging parents. Deep down we *feel* we are doing something wrong—in effect, we are ignoring what our DNA tells us we *should* be doing. And, too, society scorns people who neglect their parents. It's a universal value. That's why, just as we *feel outraged* at child abuse, we *feel outraged* when vulnerable seniors are taken advantage of or neglected.

"Respect your elders by *showing care* for your elders" is Mother Nature's stern admonition.

"Everyone Is a Critic," Says Mother Nature

You might get upset at your partner or your boss because you feel they are always criticizing you. This is probably true, but don't take it personally, because they are hardwired to criticize you, frequently.

Countless studies by social psychology colleagues demonstrate that the first and most important judgments that are made about another person are evaluative: good or bad, cold or warm, nice or mean, friendly or hostile. We pick up many other types of information, but the primary judgment we make is either positive or negative.

This can be traced to the fact that the mechanisms that integrate your brain's software with its hardware are highly emotional in nature. Your brain evolved in this manner because emotional information helps you adapt to your environment. Positive evaluations tell you the situation is friendly; negative evaluations tell you the situation is unfriendly, and in the case of your ancestors, hostile was often life threatening.

Early in life you are programmed to evaluate whether a situation is hazardous or safe. Those who evaluate a situation quickly and accurately give themselves an edge. They make better decisions. Those who take too long in their evaluation, or evaluate the information inaccurately, end up in an unmanageable situation. You are hardwired to evaluate because the information evaluation evokes can protect you.

Over time, the process of making self-evaluations for our own survival became directed to others, for the intent of helping them survive and develop, too. Parents inevitably realized that by providing evaluative information to their children, perhaps about their hunting skills or their grooming habits, gave them an edge. The same is true for clan leaders—providing evaluative information to their hunting party developed their skills and tactics and, thus, enhanced the robustness of the clan. Partners, too, came to see that by providing evaluative information to their mate—what they liked, what they disliked—became a way to strengthen their bond. Bedmates who failed to provide this information to each other became the forerunners to the term "divorcee."

Yet, the majority of people—bosses, parents, husbands, and wives—experience *getting criticism* to be anxiety arousing, especially when it is mismanaged, accompanied by angry and sarcastic tones.

Being an expert on "giving and taking criticism," I would conclude that the reasons for these bad reactions are primal memories that negative evaluations can be life threatening, and these primal memories stimulate feelings of anxiety and threat.

"Everybody is a critic," says Mother Nature, but not everyone is a good critic. To be a *positive critic*, remember that the purpose of providing evaluative information is to help a person. Keep in mind: *criticism intent*.

The next time you criticize your children's homework, remember that the intent of your criticism is to teach them and build their confidence, not undermine it. The next time you criticize an employee, remember your intent is to help him develop so that he can do better next time—be improvement-oriented. And, remember, the next time you criticize your partner, the intent of your criticism is to share with her about how you think the relationship can be enhanced, not what she is doing wrong, not to shame or blame her. In all these cases, you want to protect the other person's self-esteem.

When you incorporate Mother Nature's intent into your criticisms, people will know that you do it because you care.

Community Caring

It would be an honor to Mother Nature if we were to become a more nurturing and caring society. Talk is cheap, so Mother Nature would consider only actions honorable.

First, we need more awareness and acknowledgment of acts of care giving in our society. Right now, too many people, especially in the working world, perceive the world as a hostile place and that human nature is selfish and aggressive. We are suspicious of good behavior, and think it is motivated by self-aggrandizing intentions. Somebody makes a donation, and we immediately think they did it for the tax break or the "patrons" plaque on the wall. We need to change this perception by getting the message out that we are hard-wired to make positive gestures to others, to nurture others. Promoting the perception that people and societies are inherently care giving will have profound life-enhancing effects for everyone. We need more presidents to write about the importance of giving.

Since care giving starts with the mother-infant relationship, it would honor Mother Nature if all mothers had equal access to good health care. Ensuring a healthy pregnancy helps not only the mother and her child, but also our society as a whole. Yet, the United States is one of the few nations in the developed world that lacks a national health program. Pregnant women are left to arrange their own prenatal care. Those with insurance get it, and those without insurance make do with whatever clinic services are available. This is more than a slap in the face to Mother Nature, it is a national disgrace.

Our redemption would occur if we make sure that, regardless of income, all expectant mothers have equal access to the resources that will enhance their pregnancy. For example, some communities offer mother-mentors to "at-risk" young women from low economic and social classes. These programs are found to reduce the stress of the expectant mother by providing support and education that helps her be a better caregiver to her newborn.

Increasing the care giving in our institutions would also honor Mother Nature. In the business world, this means training and educating employees in the skills that help them relate to each other in more supportive and encouraging ways, and to have flexible policies that are sensitive to employee needs. Our education system can be more care giving by maximizing cooperative learning, teaching children conflict resolution skills, and providing constant developmental opportunities for teachers—their own development helps them develop the young. Our criminal justice system, too, needs to be more care giving—not more lenient, but more effective in efforts to rehabilitate offenders so that they leave destructive paths behind and are supported on a constructive life course.

All these actions would honor Mother Nature for giving us the nurturing instinct. The Plaque would read as follows:

To Mother Nature

Who taught us all that it is better to give than to receive.

Part IV

Beautify...So You Can Pull People Toward You

Enhance your life by using your attraction instincts

12

Pulling People Toward You

Your Evolutionary Heritage

Silverback gorillas, both male and female, spend a good amount of their day in grooming activities to look and smell good. They bathe in the river, clean and polish their teeth with their nails, and spend hours grooming their pelts.

The gorillas' emphasis on physical attractiveness—even when they are not mating—serves the purpose of making themselves desirable to each other. The more attractive the gorillas are to each other, the more they stay together as a cohesive unit.

Beauty Attracts

All the universal things we term beauty, that we deem attractive, can be traced to survival. When fruit is immature and useless as seed, it is green and inconspicuous against the foliage. When it ripens, it colors and gives off a sweet fragrance to attract birds and insects that will transport its seeds to fertile soil. While the fruit tree was evolving its color and scent signals, we were evolving the response that the contrast of red or peach against the green was beautiful, and the sweet scent told us it would be ripe and juicy.

Beauty's evolutionary function is to pull living things toward itself. A fruit tree evolved to *attract* pollinators. We evolved to notice and appreciate fruit when it is ripe so we could feast on it.

Symmetry, too, is a universal component of beauty. A symmetrical dwelling is a sturdier dwelling and a more attractive dwelling. People with symmetrical facial features and bodies are more beautiful than those with asymmetrical bodies, so it is only natural that those who preferred symmetry had healthier children and lived longer in their safe shelters.

At the biological level, beauty serves a natural selection sexual function: If members of a species were not attracted to each other, there would be no sexual behavior, and extinction would be swift and final.

More broadly, the evolutionary idea behind our attractive instincts contemporized is to present ourselves/work/organizations in such a way that others are drawn toward us/our work/our organization and help secure our ecological niche. Deftly applied, the genius of your attractive instincts helps you do this.

All things being equal, the more attractive job candidate makes the score. More to the point, if you don't want the job, make yourself as *unattractive* as possible. A presentation using the latest technology is typically rated higher than the same content presented in a less eye-catching format. It speaks to primal *likeability*. For example, during a cutback, your boss is told to eliminate 20 percent of the staff who are performing at the same level. You can bet the ones to stay on the payroll are the ones she likes the most. Thus, check your likeability quotient.

The ability to *beautify*, maximize one's attractiveness, gives us an edge, whether it is in a job interview, at a party, during a presentation, or while building a business.

Beauty or the Beast?

Importantly, the silverback gorilla's emphasis on attractiveness is a constant—not just a behavior during mating season. Gorillas always want to look good; it is as if looking good is something that gives them pride.

Wanting to look good must be part of our evolutionary heritage because it is the rare person who does not like to feel attractive or be desired. While millions of people strive to make themselves and their work attractive, an equal amount—or maybe even more—is disconnected with their attractive instincts—turning in sloppy work or having offensive hygiene and personalities. How can this be? I'll share with you some of the reasons I have found to explain why people become the beast instead of the beauty.

It Shouldn't Matter

"Beauty is only skin deep" might be factually correct, but to say beauty "shouldn't matter" is ridiculously incorrect. One of my potential dissertation topics was how a patient's physical attractiveness affected even his medical diagnosis. Research suggested that given the same medical history, good-looking patients got a better prognosis than those the doctor deemed "unattractive." And hundreds of psychology studies show the social benefits of being physically attractive. Yet almost all of us have been given contradictory messages that foster disconnection with our attraction instinct.

Consider the generic blind date line: "He/she has a great personality, really smart and sweet."—is code for he's short, she's not pretty, that physical attractiveness is not their strong suit, and it shouldn't matter because they have a great personality. If you do say that looks are important, there is a good chance you'll get a negative response: "You're superficial."

Parents teach their children that it's the "inner beauty" that counts—how sensitive a person is, that a person's character is more important than how they look. These might be your beliefs, but they do not negate that physical attractiveness and beauty is key to drawing others to us.

When you are told over and over that physical attractiveness shouldn't matter, that your substance is what counts, you inevitably become disconnected from making yourself glitter, from the way you dress to the way you handle yourself at work. True, all that glitters is not gold, but it is also true that the glitter gets others to look for the gold.

Attractiveness Is Physical Attractiveness

Unfortunately, most people think of attractiveness in the physical realm only. It's easy to see where this message comes from. When was the last time you saw a magazine with an "ugly model" gracing the cover? Many fine actors and actresses are nondescript—they're termed *character actors*—but movie stars are the most stunningly beautiful humans on the planet. We're bombarded by the "beauty message" constantly. Magazines, fad diets, makeover shows—all tell us how important it is to "beauty up."

As a result, we put our energy into the physical realm of beauty (which inevitably fades) and neglect the other parts of ourselves that actually can become more attractive. More people, for example, sweat it out at the gym to become more *physically* attractive rather than "work out" at the library to become more *mentally* attractive.

Tunnel vision on physical attractiveness prevents you from developing other realms of attractiveness, such as a positive attitude, that can pull people toward you. Spending hours making your PowerPoint presentation snap, crackle, and pop is fine, but not if you forget to make the content excel.

Unattractively Aware

You'd be amazed at how many people in counseling ask for tips on how to tell a person at work that he has body odor or that her work wardrobe is sloppy, skimpy, or inappropriate. I am also asked frequently for advice on how to tell an executive that his interpersonal demeanor is repellant—cold, superior, abrupt, dismissive, even "too vague." Many of us have become disconnected from our attraction instinct because no one ever tells us that the way we present ourselves and our work is unattractive.

We hesitate to tell people—especially a boss—about their unattractiveness because we find it embarrassing, or we think it will wound their feelings or spark negative repercussions—a retaliatory attitude. These reactions are likely, in fact. And if this holds you back, it is most likely true for others, so they might resist telling you that the way you dress is in bad taste or that your "slangy" way of talking with customers is unprofessional. It's no wonder that executives who are universally seen as "abrasive" or "defensive to criticism" are seldom aware of it until they are fired.

One solution from instinctual disconnection here is to be more like the silverback gorilla—tuned in to always being aware of what makes you attractive and what makes you unattractive to others—at home and at work.

Another solution to counter instinctual disconnection is to beautify.

13

Beautify Today

If you are one peach among dozens hanging on a tree, your chances for being selected by someone increase if you are gorgeous, fragrant, and ripe. If you are a puppy up for adoption among your littermates, you will probably be chosen if you are not only healthy and beautiful, but also affectionate to your siblings and playing nice with them.

The purpose of beauty is to make yourself more desirable in the eyes of others so that individuals and opportunities that enhance your life will come your way. I'll use the term *beautify* for the strategic evolutionary skill that helps you do this—make yourself more appealing, personally and interpersonally.

Your Personal Best

In one of my favorite movies, one of my favorite actors is given the task of shaping up a bunch of undisciplined and slovenly marines. First order of business is haircuts and appropriate attire with the message, "When you look like Marines, you will feel like marines. And when you feel like Marines, you will *act* like Marines."

I would agree, especially when I remember my own early clinical internship experiences with hospitalized schizophrenics in a VA Hospital. For the most part, this patient population wandered around the ward in their pajamas and robes, shuffling in slippers, with little awareness to their personal grooming. Then, the ward was taken over by a psychologist who, like the marine drill instructor, shaped these patients up. He began with personal appearance. Out with the PJs and slippers, in with neat civilian clothes and running shoes. Showers every morning. Out with the dirty, scraggly hair and beards. In with regular trips to the barbershop.

To cut to the chase, as I witnessed the patients' increased awareness of how they presented themselves physically, I noted that they immediately started to feel better about themselves. Next, they became more sociable with each other. There is now a lot of data to suggest that positive personal grooming habits are associated with positive feelings about oneself including confidence, and confidence is crucial in pulling others toward you.

The clear message from nature is that maximizing your attractiveness begins with your physical grooming. Forget about looking like a movie star—few of us do. But you can all present yourself in the best light possible—*your physical best*.

You might be significantly overweight, but you can still tuck in your shirt and wear clothes that flatter you—if you are aware. You hair might not be like Goldilocks' but you can still style it so it looks less beastly. You might not have to attend a meeting with your staff or see a client, but when you walk around the office, you might be smart to ask yourself how others perceive your appearance—is it the professional image you want to project? Be like the financial advisor who told me that every time he goes out, he asks himself, "If I bumped into a client, would I look successful?"

From this point on, begin to structure some "beauty up" time into your day, even if it is brushing your teeth in the afternoon before a meeting or having a shoe shine at least once a week. Help your kids develop attractive habits by making sure they have enough time to beauty up before school. And when you see your partner making the effort to dress and style his hair and make the home more beautiful, praise him for doing so, unless you want to be with a partner who lets himself "go."

Spending time and effort (it requires both) is mandatory to being your physical best. Silverback gorillas spend the time and make the effort, and this is a good lesson to take from them.

Improve Your Likeability Quotient

Likeability—it's a key predictor to success in all areas of life. From being the teacher's pet to party invitations to job promotions, likeability can get you where you want to go. Likeability pulls people toward you, so a good way to maximize your success is to develop attributes that increase your likeability quotient. Mother Nature generously provides some tips.

The Sense of Humor

Your ancestors who had the keenest senses of seeing and hearing probably were at the top of the clan in hunting skills, but, all things being equal, those who developed a sense of humor too became the chieftains. Two points explain why.

The first is the mental and physical benefits of positive emotions. Laughing, for example, triggers the release of *endorphins*—hormones and enzymes that are natural painkillers for your body. When we laugh, we feel good, and when we feel good, we are more productive in our work, better partners, and more loving parents. Humor's evolutionary function is to make both ourselves and the people around us *feel good*.

Now the second point. Studies—under the rubric of *emotional contagion*—indicate that nature has provided creatures the capacity to transmit moods to each other, no doubt for the purpose of communication. In humans, for example, emotional communication between mother and infant begins within days through facial expressions and range of sounds. You know by the *tone* of a person's voice when she's irritable and by the smile on a person's face that he's in a good mood.

Emotions are contagious. I'm asked, "How do you deal with a negative person? They bring everybody down." Yes, they do and that is because their negativity is contagious. It is not a coincidence that many partners of depressed mates inevitably find themselves depressed too—they are "catching" the emotions of their partners just like a bad cold.

Happily, humor is also contagious. This is why many television shows have laugh tracks—to *mood infect* you with positive feelings.

Back on the Savannah, when things got tough, who would you want to be with—the clansman who turned gloomy or the one who made you laugh? Because your human nature is to want to feel good and because humor is contagious, you would (as your ancestors did) gravitate to the caveman who transmitted positive emotions, and this would be the one with a good sense of humor. It is also fair to assume that this caveman's sense of humor would attract others, too, and inevitably, he would go on to achieve status in the community.

Hundreds of thousands of years later, I frequently hear managers and front line employees saying, "I love working for my boss. She has a great sense of humor," but I am never told, "I love working for my boss because she's depressed and irritable."

You can also make the assumption that those ancestors of yours who had a good sense of humor also attracted more than their share of desirable mates. Not only did the caveman have his status working for him, but also his sense of humor filled the air with positive emotions and pulled women toward him. Four decades of studies in the area of interpersonal attraction consistently support that among the top reasons women select their mate is for their sense of humor.

To make yourself more likeable so you can pull people toward you, connect to your sense of humor. Here are some proven effective ways to do so:

- Candid camera glasses—People-watch 5 minutes a day with the goal being to tune in to the fact that we take ourselves too seriously. Instead of feeling road rage in traffic, look at the people in the car next to you, and you are sure to gain perspective. It is a way to lighten up.
- Humor breaks—Take a daily 5-minute break to think of things that make you laugh. You will feel enthused and feel your stress melt away.
- Formal joke sessions—You will have to get out of your comfort zone to start each team meeting with a team member sharing a joke, but numerous companies have told me it brings enthusiasm into the workplace.

Speak UP!

The evolutionary function of assertiveness is to express the thoughts and feelings that can enhance you, your marriage, and your organization. This means that *assertiveness* is the furthest thing from being a pop psychology buzzword.

Just as today's organization holds a meeting to discuss the problems that threaten its ecological niche, so, too, your ancestors held similar clan conclaves to discuss the problems that threatened the clan's existence. The early man and woman who perceived that speaking up and expressing their ideas could help their tribe developed a distinct edge over their more reticent relatives.

Inevitably, those who asserted their advice and guidance on how best to meet the challenges of the day rose to positions of leadership, especially when their advice led to good results. Naturally they gravitated to those who knew the score, and more importantly, spoke their views with knowledge and confidence.

In today's world, we often confuse assertiveness with *aggressiveness*. No doubt there was a time when aggressive behavior served your ancestors well—in an individual survival situation or at war with another clan. But inevitably, as social interaction increased, aggressive "communication" lost its competitive edge. One reason might be that an aggressive style stifled the contributions of others. As a result, new thoughts on how to adapt and innovate did not surface, and the clan became extinct.

The rule at hand: Aggressiveness is getting your needs met at the expense of others, whereas assertiveness is simply an expression of your thoughts/needs/feelings with the understanding that your ideas may or may not win acceptance.

Aggressive people in the workplace usually get stalled in their careers, and aggressive kids in school usually become "problems." Constant interrupting of others in a team meeting and cutting in front of others in the lunch line are signs of an aggressive interpersonal style. A boss who bullies his staff into accepting his position might get what he wants, but in the long run, his team is suppressed. The lunchroom bully might be first in the cafeteria line but probably doesn't get invited to any birthday parties.

In contrast, there are many benefits to being assertive, including feeling better about yourself, better health, diminished stress, and improved relationships with others. All these factors make you more attractive. Accordingly, natural selection would favor assertive individuals over aggressive individuals. Practice assertive behavior by

- Use "I think/feel" statements to acknowledge your subjectivity, rather than treating your views as facts.
- Use a tone of voice that communicates respect to others.
- Make requests rather than demands.
- Listen nondefensively to the responses of others.
- Show appreciation that your views were listened to.

Praise—Early, Early, Early, Early Behaviorism

Long ago, parents figured out that it was important to praise their kids for behaviors that increased their odds for survival, such as vigilance and looking both ways before they broke cover, or looking before they leaped into the terrain below. Parents who encouraged caution had children who survived longer, as they would become less prone to misfortunes caused by carelessness. The leader of the hunting party who praised the newest recruit for his stealth in sneaking up on the prey increased the likelihood that the young man would become a good hunter.

These are both examples of the evolutionary function of *praise*— to reinforce the behaviors that give a person that competitive edge. It is easy to see why praising others helps them, but how does praising others help you become more attractive?

As your ancestral parents learned more about the behaviors that would further secure their child's ecological niche, they naturally praised their children when they exhibited these positive behaviors. Soon, the youngsters realized that doing these behaviors was making them more competent. This built their confidence and self-esteem, and they experienced positive feelings. So it came to pass, praise led to competence and competence led to confidence.

Because these behaviors pleased the parent, it was only natural that the parent expressed approval with the most loving tones. Through the process of emotional contagion, the child was infected with the positive feelings of the parent. Numerous studies show that children who receive praise from their parents, in turn have positive feelings toward their parents. In other words, parents make themselves more attractive to their kids by praising them.

The same holds true in today's work arena: When employees are praised, productivity and morale go up, and the manager is perceived more favorably—the manager becomes more attractive.

Praising others is not the end-all, but any mother would tell you that it does make you less beastly.

Listen Well

It's easy to see how natural selection favors those who listen well. Two cavemen out for a walk, and you can bet the one who returned was the one who "heard" the leopard stalking them. Hundreds of thousands of years later, *listening well* still enhances your edge and likeability.

I'm sure you've been to meetings where it seems like nobody is using their ears, and I am sure you have had family discussions where everyone talks over each other. I'm just as sure that, at times, you have felt that your partner is not listening to you. The results? Bad decisions, chaos, and conflict.

Listening is a fundamental survival tool. By listening you collect data to solve problems and innovate, and you also strengthen interpersonal bonds. Good listeners are sought-after leaders. Think about those who learned to *listen to the people*. Listening to their needs enabled them to serve the people. In every profession and interaction—parent, lover, therapist, doctor, lawyer, or Indian chief—listening well is elemental. It also bonds us to the person who respects us enough to listen to our ideas.

Make yourself more attractive by listening to others. Some points to remember:

- Do not interrupt others; doing so indicates you are not listening.
- Respond to what people say rather than initiate a new topic.
- Validate your understanding by paraphrasing or summarizing what you think the person is communicating.
- When you are not sure you understand, gently probe for more information and ask for clarification.
- Remember the function of listening is to collect data so that you can help people enhance their lives.

Looking your physical best, having a sense of humor, being assertive, and listening to and praising others are tools that nature has given us so that we can make ourselves more attractive to others and thereby enhance our lives in all of our arenas.

14

Broadly Attractive

I've bet you've never been described as *broadly attractive*, or for that matter, used the expression to describe someone else. Yet, this is the phrase an evolutionary understanding posits to help you take advantage of the genius of your instincts.

How can you make yourself attractive in the different "habitats" of your life? Here are some recommendations from Mother Nature.

Becoming a More Attractive Mate

I was in Las Vegas speaking at a conference for insurance agents. I had been asked to speak to the agents' spouses. The day before my presentation, I was in an elevator with a group of people (most wearing the company's badge). As we began to climb, I overheard a conversation between a wife and her husband in which she berated him for losing a few dollars in the casino. It would be the example that I would use to introduce the subject of my presentation, the importance of being a *supportive spouse*, and according to Mother Nature, one of the keys to becoming an attractive mate and maintaining the love of your partner.

Flash back to the young man coming home from a hunt. "I didn't do well. I caught nothing. Everyone else got something." The cavewoman who stroked his face soothingly and said, "Don't worry. You will be the best tomorrow. I know you will. I believe you will," was supporting him and strengthening their bond. The woman who retorted "You caught nothing? How could you catch nothing?" drove him away. A few hundred thousand years later, when these couples' descendants are attending the conference in Las Vegas, which couple do you think is having a better time?

Being supportive to your spouse when he is feeling down or has experienced a setback rebuilds his confidence, and this confidence and the positive feelings it breeds fuels his belief that he can rebound and be successful tomorrow. This is one of the evolutionary functions of support—*it helps people recover from adversity, thus increasing their chances to survive*. Being a supportive mate make you more attractive because over time, the supportive spouse *is felt* as a confidence-builder.

We like to *feel confident*, so it is only natural that we would be attracted to people who build our confidence. "I couldn't have done it without my husband/wife," is homage to the supportive spouse. And there is overwhelming contemporary research indicating that marital discord is often rooted in a lack of support.

How do you express support? One way is to be encouraging— make direct statements to your spouse that you believe in her ability to be successful in her endeavors. Be a positive thinker *for* your spouse. Another way is to simply listen.

Being *dependable* is also part of Mother Nature's advice for making yourself attractive. As your ancestral clans evolved, male and female roles started to take form, inevitably leading to a gender-based division of labor. For each husband/wife unit to flourish, each party relied on each other for the accomplishment of specific tasks. Imagine that you had a successful hunt and your share is a juicy haunch of bison. You hand it over to your mate, take a nap, and wake up hungry, only to find out that your woman hasn't even started the cook fire. Or worse yet, while she was next door gossiping, the dog stole it. It's a bad night, and it becomes worse the next day when your friend tells you about the savory stew his own woman prepared.

Of course, it's true in reverse, as well. Cavewoman prepares all day for her man to return, and not only is he late, he is empty-handed. You can imagine how she feels when she hears her friend the next day tell how her partner's hunting party came home with a week's supply of prime ribs.

These examples are simplistic, but they do show the evolutionary function of dependability—to show another person we can be relied on to do tasks needed for the family to flourish. An inconsistent hunter is not going to attract as many mates as the dependable one. In today's world, this concern would be voiced by a mother to her daughter as, "Can he make a decent living?"

When your mate perceives you as being dependable, your desirability increases because your mate comes to rely on you. Over time, this reliance turns into trust, and I'm sure that you are not surprised to learn that numerous studies show that trustworthiness is a highly desirable trait.

You can begin to increase your dependability by honoring your smallest daily commitments. If you told your mate you'd mail a letter for her, do it. If you said you would save a certain part of your paycheck, put it in the bank and show her how the balance is growing. Show your partner he can rely on you, and you will find yourself becoming more attractive in his eyes. Later on, you will see how dependability is actually hardwired into you and how it is integrated into your other instinctual tools, too.

One more piece of attraction advice: Increase your *emotional communication*. Recall the evolutionary function of emotions—they communicate information that helps us survive, solve problems, and enrich our lives. Since we are hardwired with emotions, it follows that communicating your emotions to your partner is important, as well as picking up on your partner's emotional messages to you.

Ancestors who could read the face of fear in those running from a predator had a head start on those who needed to be told to run, and those who could interpret the nonverbal signs of hurt in their mates were more prone to comfort them—so they could recover their confidence.

If a husband picks up that his wife is anxious about an interview, he can help her prepare. If a wife senses her husband is angry, she can gently probe for the reasons and then help problem solve and restore his equilibrium.

Increase your awareness to the emotional cues your partner sends outs. How do you know when he is angry, anxious, or dejected? Can you read it in his face and body language? Can you hear the tones in your partner's voice?

Does your partner freely reveal intimate thoughts and feelings to you? How comfortable are you in doing the same? When each partner feels comfortable in expressing thoughts and feelings, the relationship can be strengthened because the issues that threaten the relationship can be nipped in the bud.

Communicating your true, unvarnished emotions and thoughts creates intimacy, and your own disclosures make it easier for your partner to be intimate and trusting, as well. In our contemporary psychological world, this is called *authentic communication*. We like to be with people we can "be real" with or express ourselves in an authentic manner. We are attracted to them.

Being supportive, encouraging, and dependable and using authentic communication are Mother Nature's beauty tips for becoming a more attractive partner.

Come Home for Thanksgiving

I've never met parents who didn't want their kids to be close, loving, and attracted to them. You have *parental attractiveness* if your children naturally come to you when they are in trouble, when they did something wrong, and when they feel down.

From an evolutionary perspective, it's easy to discern the survival function of being attractive to your kids. It allows you to further the advancement of *your* children, which increases the chance your life line will persist.

If, for example, your children feel you accept them, and your intent is always to help them, they will be *attracted* to you. They will come to you in time of need and, thus, give you the opportunity to provide support, advice, and help that allows them to meet the challenge at hand.

However, if your children—whether they are 5 years old or 25—perceive you as being nonaccepting and critical, they are more likely to keep their problems from you and rarely ask for help. Consequently, you lose the opportunity to help them succeed.

Those ancestral parents who were able to pull their children toward them were able to give their kids a competitive edge. Those who couldn't were unable to help their family line continue.

Despite the evolutionary advantage that parental attractiveness gives you, too many parents work against this goal by the way they respond when their children initially begin to confide in them—they *judge* what their child did, and most of the time, it is a negative evaluation. "You shouldn't have lost your jacket." "How could you forget your books at soccer practice?"

Of course, such negative evaluations are accompanied by angry tones. Later on, when a daughter informs a parent about a significant choice she's made, the response is often, "Are you sure? I'm surprised. I think you are making a mistake." And these responses carry emotional tones too, usually disappointment and anxiety, which, through emotional contagion, are picked up by the child. Because these feelings are unpleasant, and because it is human nature to feel good, it is understandable why so many children avoid their parents even when they need them.

The parental evolutionary tool that helps is *nonevaluative listening*. It means that when your kids share their problems, dilemmas, feelings, or issues, your *attractive response* is to help them reflect on their feelings, clarify their thoughts, and teach them the *tool of problem solving*. This engages rather than pushes them away. It helps create a positive parental environment for your children. You help *them* analyze the challenge, encourage *them* to come up with multiple strategies for addressing the challenge, and then allow *them* to select the best solution—to develop their competencies, experience their feelings, and confront their doubts. Nonjudgmental listening creates a safe and secure *problem-solving process* crucial to your child's personal and interpersonal development, and mental and physical health.

It's an evolutionary fact that children inevitably distance themselves from their parents. But if you are a parent who makes yourself attractive to your kids, you can count on this fact: They will always want to come home for Thanksgiving.

The Magnet of Expertise

Expertise has the obvious evolutionary function of giving you an advantage in a particular task that helps you create a niche where you are valuable to the group. Expertise in healing with herbs might have been one of the ways your ancestors secured their ecological niche. One of your relatives might be doing the same thing through expertise in radiology or auto mechanics. Expertise attracts people, and physicians, lawyers, builders, and mechanics will all testify this to be true.

Early men learned that they did not have the competencies to deal with all the challenges that threatened their existence. Once we evolved safe shelters and stable food sources, we began to evolve tools, medicine, and specialists within the clan. And we traded with other clans who had developed skills and tools our own clan hadn't "invented."

Experts achieved prominent positions in their community. People always came to them to learn. The experts always had business; imagine an expert hunter teaching skills and passing on his hunting knowledge to young hunters-to-be. Is this not a forerunner to the business seminar?

Thus, expertise has evolved into an *attractive mechanism.* A couple is attracted to an expert financial advisor because they perceive the advisor can help secure their future. A sick man is attracted to the best doctor because she is perceived as capable of saving his life. Parents are attracted to the expert college prep course because they believe it will help their kid get into the top university. Believe Mother Nature when she tells you that expertise and quality are magnets for pulling people toward you.

To follow Mother Nature's recommendation here, you would be wise to take two steps. The first is to *always be in the process of enhancing your expertise.* This is a requirement to be two cuts above the norm. Reading journals, attending seminars, studying after work, and obtaining graduate degrees might be a hassle, but they are avenues to maximizing and updating your expertise.

Second, do not be shy: *Let others know you are an expert.* In fact, Mother Nature would elaborate this point in her marketing class: *Make your expertise your major competitive edge.* On your resume, detail your training, education, and expertise. In the context of product, expertise translates to quality, so the advice would be: Make the *quality of your product* your major competitive edge, as natural selection chooses the best.

A Beautiful Place to Work

Long before there were management "gurus," Mother Nature spelled out the qualities of an "attractive corporate culture"—one that would attract the best and the brightest, retain the best and the brightest, and thus continually have a strong ecological niche.

In a nourishing, desirable corporate culture or "habitat," ideas are expressed freely, great work is rewarded, emotions are expressed and managed effectively, employees feel supportive and listened to, and individuals feel they are growing.

Mother Nature adds one more component: *flexibility*. Hunting parties that noticed that the trail they were on was leading away from water holes and grassland changed their courses to find the likelier locations of antelope. Those who blindly stuck to the trail came back hungry. A quarterback changes the play at the line of scrimmage when he sees an unexpected defensive alignment. His flexibility allows him to pick up a first down.

Those on the Savannah who learned the adaptation of being flexible (developed in your neo-cortex) gave themselves an edge, since they could more quickly adapt in real time. Many times, their flexibility helped others. So, of course, flexibility led to respect and status. I bet you don't like to be with or work with "rigid" people. I will double my bet that you enjoy people who are flexible in their behaviors, choices, and how they respond to you. Companies and organizations that are flexible remain successful. If you have learned from evolution, you are always interacting and responding—adapting rather than staying static and becoming extinct.

Foster flexibility in your organization culture via management, strategy, decision making, training, and customer service.

Humor, listening, praise, trustworthiness, and flexibility are the components of attraction. If this sounds familiar, it should. Mother Nature has been advocating these attributes for hundreds of thousands of years, because they work. This also reiterates a theme of the book: Let's look to the past and see the success rules that have worked for hundreds of thousands of years.

Beauty or the Beast

Reconnect with your attraction instinct so that you can enhance your life personally and professionally. Remember, it is an evolutionary fact that beauty attracts and beast repels, so all you need to do is decide: Do you want to be the Beauty or the Beast?

Part V

Co-op...So You Can Get People Working Together

Enhance your life by using your cooperative instincts

15

Team Game

Your Evolutionary Heritage

Canadian geese migrate thousands of miles twice a year in flocks with wonderfully integrated movement. The long axis of the flock is at almost right angles to the direction of the movement—the flock is roughly shaped like a great bird. Each goose lifts and lowers its wings in sync with the bird on either side of it, flying as one great bird.

This is an example of a behavior in which two or more animals act as one, with both individual and group benefits. In the case of the geese, the formation reduces drag and creates draft, so the long migration isn't as tiring as a solo flight would be, thus ensuring more the group (and thus individuals) would have a successful flight. Such cooperation is to ensure the integration and coordination of system components, whether it is a wolf pack, a football team, or a media conglomerate, so that tasks can be achieved smoothly and efficiently. Cooperative efforts are mandatory to building both permanent and short-term organizations. Our co-op instinct stimulates cooperation.

If you had to listen to a pep talk on the subject of cooperation or the more popular term, teamwork, you'd be smart to take notes if the speaker was Mother Nature. Unlike any of the other speakers, she would start to make her point by telling you about the first team—the very first team.

The First Team

The first life on earth was individual, but it was literally only a matter of time before it realized that it needed others to survive, so it teamed up with its fellow particles to form the first team. This proved to be a winning move, and ever since, Mother Nature has declared life to be a team game.

Zoologists tell us three and half billion years ago you'd find a team of 1,000 genes running bacteria 5 millionths of a millimeter long. A billion years ago, you'd find complex cells a million times heavier than bacteria and run by teams of 10,000 genes or more: the protozoa. By 500 million years ago, the planet saw complex bodies made up of a billion cells. The trilobite, an arthropod the size of a mouse, was the largest animal on the planet. Ever since then, the model has been bigger and better. The largest animal that has ever lived on earth—the blue whale, with 100,000 trillion cells—still swims the oceans today. The largest plant, the Giant Sequoia, still thrives majestically, as well.

Clearly, the first's atom's instinct to work with others was a smart play. Your own body is testimony—from the genes that team up to form chromosomes to the complex cells that team up to form bodies. Cooperation was the game to play then and is still the game to play today.

Project management, whether for an advertising campaign or a wedding, requires cooperation. So does scoring a touchdown, making your connecting flight, and getting your package delivered to the overseas client. Big game hunting among your ancestors, raising your children, having a satisfying marriage, maintaining community standards, buying your house, and working in a profitable company all require cooperation, as does living in a lawful and productive society. We live in a world that has evolved and is governed by cooperation, so it is no wonder that *you are hardwired to be cooperative*—it not only enhances your life, it makes your life possible.

Yet, despite its life-enhancing effects, the world on both micro and macro levels is plagued by the systemic *lack of cooperation.* In counseling sessions, I'd hear (dozens of times) each partner accusing the other of being selfish. In the working world, I've encountered many individuals who are relentlessly competitive with their fellow workers to the point of hurting the team. And you'd have to live on another planet to not know that few countries cooperate with each other (but those that do reap benefits).

While we all know cooperation is vital to our lives, how is it that people become so disconnected with this instinct? No matter how you spin it, it is because you are selfish.

Selfish Jean

Selfish Jean is all around—in your home, at work, in your community. She is best and most simply described, in contemporary vernacular, as someone who is "looking out for number one," even when it is at the expense of others. All sorts of teams—from marriage to corporate—break up because of Selfish Jean.

Have you ever met a Selfish Jean? Anybody who has met you has, because each one of us is made up of selfish *genes*.

The *selfish gene* refers to the now widely accepted evolutionary and biological idea that people consistently do not engage in behaviors for the good of their group, family, or at times themselves. Rather, people do things that benefit their own genes. There is no moral attachment to the selfish concept (although people do respond to the morality of the idea)—it is simply a way of saying that your genes are hardwired to further themselves, to go on as long as possible; this is evidenced by the fact often pointed out by biologists: None of your ancestors were celibate.

Frequently, the individual and genetic interest coincides, but not always. Bees die in the act of stinging; salmon die after they spawn. Many times, the interests of the genes urge a creature to act in a way that benefits its offspring, such as leaving a child a large inheritance. But here, too, there are exceptions, such as when a bird deserts its chicks after a drought devastates the water and food supply. At other times, the gene's interest is best served by doing things for the benefit of other relatives, like worker ants that help the queen breed to secure the next generation. In other examples from nature, the gene interest dictates behavior that benefits the group as a whole—musk oxen circling shoulder to shoulder to protect their young from the enemy wolf pack, or penguins huddling in shifts against the polar chill. Regardless of the common benefit, the innate selfish gene, without exception, operates on the principle that living things are designed to do things that enhance the chances of their genes or copies of their genes surviving and replicating.

The concept goes on to point out that since genes are the replicating currency of natural selection, it is a mathematical certainty that genes that incite survival behavior win out over genes that do not. Thus, the previous and common perception of social scientists that an ant colony was a complex cooperative society in which everybody was working together for the good of the group turned out to be an illusion.

From the gene's perspective, the altruistic behavior of the worker ant is completely and clearly selfish. By doing its job in the colony, each ant is pushing for its genetic eternity—through the queen's royal offspring, its brother and sisters, rather than its own offspring. It's the same as when a bee sacrifices its life to protect the hive. It's a brave act, but the bee does so to ensure that its genes "in the hive" continue to thrive. In effect, the ants and bees are doing their job with the same gene-selfishness that humans use when fighting their rivals for that plum promotion.

Could it be that every act of selfishness is simply a moment when our selfish genes are galvanized for their innate purpose? After all, are not all your selfish acts simply protecting, at some level, your own interest? I don't think it is a stretch to say that acts of selfishness are manifestations of selfish genes, and selfish genes would certainly disconnect us from our cooperative instincts.

There is much more to say about the selfish gene but the most relevant point here is that despite its competitive nature, it does have the capability to be a team player and do well for the good of the group.

In other words, the lesson is that selfish *genes succeed because they do cooperate*—but they have to be managed.

Gene Management

Any team coach or department head will tell you that it is hard enough getting a team to pull together, but it becomes exceedingly difficult when each team member has a competitive nature. It's only a matter of time, they would say, before somebody wants more, to be the star, "the straw that stirs the drink." An effective manager knows how to harness the competitiveness among team members so that they can work as one.

Consider the social organization of a bee colony. Only the queen has the "right" to reproduce. Worker bees are also able to reproduce, but for the most part, this is latent. They are nature's "Plan B" if the queen dies. Nature tells us that each peasant female bee is hardwired to reproduce. You would think a few selfish or "rogue" bees would breed as much as possible—but they don't. Why not?

The answer is that each worker bee is loyal to the queen bee because each one is her direct offspring. Thus, the bees end up monitoring themselves in a system designed to prevent selfish worker bees from acting on their instincts. Any egg not marked with a special pheromone by the queen is eaten by the workers, all in the name of serving the common good. In other words, the harmony of the hive is achieved only by suppressing the selfishness of individuals. The pheromone "logo"—this is a queen bee product, not a knockoff—is the mechanism that creates cooperation, another hardwiring job by Mother Nature.

Humans lack this special pheromone, but Mother Nature did evolve another mechanism common to all humans that helps us all manage selfishness and work for the common good. The evolved mechanism is your large brain, or more specifically, the social part of your brain, the neo-cortex.

Your Big Brain Is a Socialite

The most dramatic feature that separates the human species from other animals is a big brain that features a large neo-cortex, the center of social reasoning. Much larger animals, such as hippos and elephants, have much smaller brains relative to their size than we do.

Why do we have a big brain? Some would say due to our technological needs. Others posit it is to meet our complex nutritional needs. But the data to support these theories and others is unconvincing.

Scientists from multiple disciplines now believe the reason for our large brain is that, more than any other species, we are socialites. We live by our ability to coordinate our needs with those around us. Our entire success as a species arises from our *social wiring*.

The need to cooperate seems to have driven the evolution of our big brain, and it is easy to see how natural selection would favor those who had greater brain power, as greater brain power immediately would make both sexes better at their jobs.

Men first. In the hunting era, a greater ability to plan, manipulate, deceive, and evaluate were mental capacities that boosted men's ability to bring down their prey, defeat their enemies, and form strategic coalitions. Furthermore, hunting success provided greater and more consistent sources of protein, and this, in turn, gave them better health and greater opportunities to have healthy offspring. It also meant that people could live closer together because there was a more consistent and ample food supply. More people living together increased social interaction, necessitating greater social skills so tribes could grow into communities. The social skills required—developing values and rules and establishing a system of justice—increased the need for brain power, too.

Sexual selection also favored "big brain hunters." By bringing home the bacon, the good hunter increased his attractiveness and thus could become more selective in choosing his mate, so a man with a big brain had a big advantage over those whose brain lagged behind.

Women, too, had an impact on brain evolution. While men were out hunting, women were gathering food and cultivating the first gardens; making tools, shoes, and garments; and inventing improvements to make their shelters more secure and comfortable. They were also raising and teaching their children and interacting with and comforting each other. Natural selection would, of course, favor women whose brains were most socially adept.

When you combine the mental capacities required for both sexes to meet their survival tasks and to achieve productive social interaction, you can see why we have a big brain, and why for the most part it is a social brain.

Is this true? If the demands of social life have driven the evolution of brain size, there should be a corollary across the animal kingdom between the complexity of the social system and the size of the brain. There is. Brain size, especially the size of the neo-cortex, increases across primate species as you see more complex social systems. Note that if the neo-cortex is damaged, memory for people is not harmed, but social skills are grossly disrupted.

We have a social brain, and it is what helps us manage Selfish Jeans, in all of our environments.

16

Interaction: Play Ball!

Underlying all cooperative instincts is *interaction*—the joint activities/communication between two or more people in which each individual influences and is influenced by others. The more we stimulate interaction and make it a fair give and take where each person benefits individually, the bigger the payoff for the common good.

Giving and taking criticism, for example, is an interactive process: *How* you give criticism influences how your partner or coworker receives it. How he responds influences you the next time you criticize that person. Criticizing your partner or coworker productively increases the likelihood he will respond productively, and his productive response influences you to continue your productive ways. It's an interactive system—both parties use communication to enhance their relationship. In effect, your and his give and take of criticism is cooperative.

Making the interaction (be it a performance appraisal, or cleaning the house) a collaborative effort for the common good would be one way to apply your cooperative instinct.

A manager will see little happen at a meeting if he cannot stimulate interaction among the team or passively sits back and "lets them express themselves." More often than not, the group sits back, too. However, if the manager or teacher stimulates the team or class into sharing their thoughts and feelings by asking strategic questions or by starting the session off by sharing her own thoughts—throwing out the first ball—he gets the inning going.

Frequency of interaction is a huge factor, too. How often do you interact with your kids? It is hard to get them to cooperate with chores if the only time you interact is to dictate responsibilities. The same is true with your assistant and your clients. Financial advisors repeatedly voice that phoning and having their clients into the office for updates for "face time" is their key to getting client referrals and building their business. This is not surprising. The more you interact with someone, the greater the opportunity to build mutually beneficial relationships.

Simulating interaction initiates cooperation; it is Mother Nature's call: "Let's Play Ball!"

Reciprocity: The Give and Take of Cooperation

The core of your cooperative instincts is *reciprocity*, the give and take that occurs in any relationship. We all know there are times—and people—when we give more than we get. The reverse is just as true. Over the long run, though, the cooperative nature of any relationship will be a function of fair give and take.

A great deal of research has been done on the role that reciprocity plays in cooperation, and all of it affirms what Mother Nature has hardwired into our social brain, and the brains of other species, but to a lesser degree.

Reciprocity I: The Real Value of Recognition

The vampire bat is one of your teachers. Vampire bats, according to those who study them, have long-term family units, often as long as 18 years. As a result, they have *stability* in their groups, interacting with the same bats every day. Also, for their body size, like humans they have a very large neo-cortex, so it is not surprising that they have complex social relationships that feature cooperation. In fact, when it comes to reciprocity, they literally "step up to bat" so to speak. They share blood with each other as a means of helping each other out when food becomes scarce.

This behavior explains one of Mother Nature's rules for stimulating reciprocity. The first is *recognition*; the bats recognize each other. You can't repay a favor if you don't know who provided it, and you can't expect a return if others don't know whom they "owe." Recognition—others knowing you and you knowing them—is essential to cooperative play.

A smart strategy at work, especially when you are starting a new position, is to get up front and personal. Forget the advice you've heard about keeping personal matters at home. The truism is, by letting people know you personally, you increase the likelihood they will play ball with you. Self-disclosure is your friend and gives meaning to your interactions. Share stories and your interests, all for the purpose of increasing your familiarity to others. And, get to know as many people on a personal basis as possible. Personal delivery of a message, especially early in the game, is much more effective than email for getting the reciprocity game going. Remember, ineraction cultivates reciprocity.

In those huge university classes, the student who makes sure the professor knows who she is throughout the semester has a much better chance for the teacher to cooperate with her by extending her paper deadline than the student who steps forward from the last row the day before it's due. And, it will be hard for your boss to thank you or advance your career if he is clueless about what you contribute. Have you ever stimulated interaction with your boss by inviting her to lunch?

Getting others to know you *personally* is crucial to getting others to play reciprocity with you.

Reciprocity II: "But Will You Pay Me Back?"

Vampire bats teach us more about reciprocity by the nature of their blood sharing: *payback*. A vampire bat will return the blood to the giving donor but will not give blood to a bat that didn't give him any blood. While recognition starts the reciprocity game, payback is how we keep score.

Take a minute to reflect on reciprocity in your life and most likely, you will describe it in the form of paybacks, or behaviors that would cause you to "pay back" later on. Here's a litany:

- "I can't believe he won't, after all I've done."
- "They gave us an expensive wedding gift; we'll have to do the same."
- "They've had us over for dinner twice; we'd better invite them over."
- "She's only doing this because she wants me to do something for her."

The phrases change, but the message is clear: We think of reciprocity as an exchange, or even an obligation.

Payback or quality of exchange as a feature of reciprocity has been studied in many disciplines, most notably in the fields of game theory, economics, and social psychology. A common research method is putting individuals in situations that conflict their individual interest with group interest, as in the famous "prisoner" dilemma scenarios. Here, the participants are put in a situation in which each has to make specific choices. Each choice earns a set score. The game is rigged—by cooperating with each other, each participant will consistently get the most points in the long run. But, at any given time, a player can boost his score by "selling out" his opponent. The dilemma is, when one player yields to the sweet temptation of personal gain by betraying the adversary, the opponent is likely to retaliate with the same strategy: Tit for Tat. Cooperation flies out the window, following the trust that has already left the building. The end result of this scenario is that players ends up getting a significantly lower score when they play for their self-interest (or selfish genes) than if they had cooperated throughout the game.

Many of us live our lives playing Tit for Tat, always keeping score on favors and who "owes" whom. The underlying "game plan?" Give what we get, but no more. This strategy for stimulating reciprocity is far from the best. A superior strategy seems to be practiced by lions.

Lionesses live in tight-knit *prides*, each pride defending its territory against rival prides. Lionesses claim their territorial ownership by roaring. When a foreign roar is heard, the lionesses usually approach the sound to investigate, some boldly, others hesitantly. Do the lions play Tit for Tat? If they did, a courageous lioness that steps up to meet the uninvited guest should expect a reciprocal favor from the laggard who hangs back. Tit for Tat: The next time an intruder roars, the laggard should take the risk and lead. Yet, researchers would tell you this is not the case—there is no payback. The laggard might be resented, but there is no punishment. The behavior is simply accepted, and the same lioness continues to take the risk.

This behavior, mixed with game theory findings, illuminates an important point. The best strategy for creating cooperative relationships is *to continue to act cooperatively, even when others don't.*

In game theory, for example, prisoner dilemma games are set up in which different computer programs play each other. Each program is designed with a different strategy of playing Tit for Tat, with a player trying to exploit a relationship to rack up points, occasionally not cooperating to win extra points, always at the expense of the opponent. When the games end, what is the winning play?

It is not the strategy that sucks in an opponent to cooperative play, only to betray them at the very end to win. It is also not the play that is literally Tit for Tat. One betrayal often sets in motion a destructive competitive process that cannot be stopped. The winning play can best be described as Tit, Tit, Tit, for Tat. The winning play is one that is forgiving to those who have a cooperative lapse. In fact, they forgive several times. Unfailingly, the consistent cooperative and forgiving play scores the highest. The competitive players end up competing against themselves and drive each other *out of the game.* Cooperative players end up playing other cooperative players, and both flourish, just like in real life. What you learn here is that you can stimulate cooperation—get others to play reciprocity—by consistently being the good guy, at work and at home. Specifically, *be forgiving when others aren't cooperating and continue your cooperative efforts*.

"Yes, I'll Pay You Back!"

Recognition and payback influence reciprocity in another way, one that is unique to humans and made possible by your social brain: the expectation, foresight, and planning of future encounters.

Studies show that the more you anticipate future encounters with the same person, the more likely you are to be a nice guy on the grounds that in future encounters, that person will remember your good nature and be nice to you back. You are more polite, studies say, to the people in your home town who want the same table in your local restaurant than to the strangers who want the same table in a foreign city.

It's easy to see how reciprocity became a staple in your ancestor's makeup. Since they lived in groups—tribes first, growing to communities of approximately 150 people—you would interact daily with the same people. Because of the stability of the relationships, it would make sense for you to share a piece of meat with your fellow tribesmen or be happy to help them make a tool or gather some fruit since it would only be a matter of time before you needed their help in turn. And your helpful acts would earn you a "reputation" as a team player in the entire community, so developing a reputation as one who engages in reciprocity *without immediate benefits* would come in handy. When you needed a favor from a tribesman you didn't know well, your past acts would serve you well. Your reputation would make you trustworthy—the reciprocal person became one who could be depended on, one who could be trusted to cooperate and be helpful, even when there were no immediate gains. Such a reputation would elicit reciprocity from others, even in situations when *they* would receive no immediate gains. Why? Because your reputation would guarantee payback.

Developing a reputation that you could be counted on to reciprocate was a smart adaptation then and is a smart career strategy today. If you are a parent, it means letting your kids know that while they can't be lucky every day, it is smart to be nice every day because it pays off in the long run. Teach your kids the truth: Nice guys finish first.

Take a break to think about the role that reciprocity plays in your own life—how do you play the game? When your partner is in a selfish mood, are you able to act cooperatively, or do you mismanage your emotions and play Tit for Tat? How often do you help your colleagues at work when there is no immediate payback for you? If your answer is rarely, don't be surprised if their cooperation is rare. Do you honor your obligations? Do you return favors? If not, people might find you less trustworthy than you think.

Whether you are initiating a relationship or are in the midst of one, you can't enjoy the fruits of cooperation without the reciprocation of others. You can get it by taking advantage of human hardwiring: Be personable, frequently interact with key people, initiate favors to others, and develop a payback reputation. These factors helped your ancestors stimulate cooperation, and they will help you do the same.

17

Stimulating Cooperation

Our cooperative instincts and adaptations engineered the complex cultures we live in today. Mother Nature's prescription here is not to develop these instincts—you already have them. The first order of business is to *stimulate them*. The three supreme strategies are *ensuring a division of labor*, *emphasizing identity*, and *playing fair*.

Once you stimulate your instincts, you can begin to *co-op (cooperate)* by applying your instincts strategically and creatively. As you familiarize yourself with your cooperative instincts, reflect on your current use of them with friends and neighbors, family and colleagues.

Stimulate the Division of Labor

Long before the great economist discovered the economic efficiency of the *division of labor*, Mother Nature invented it with the evolution of your body. She created a group of specialists that work together for the benefit of the common good. From cells to organs, each has a job to do, and each benefits from the job performance of others. Nothing tries to do everything at once—it would be inefficient. Your legs might not like walking a mile after dinner while the stomach merely digests the delicious meal, but the end result is that they both perform their task for the good of the whole.

In groups, too, we each have our specialties to contribute. Men hunted collectively, but each man brought a specialty to the party.

While one selected saplings for spears, another perfected the technique for sharpening them in the fire. Another became adept at throwing them, and another studied kills to discover where the kill-shots should pierce the game. The same would be true for women; some became adept at gardening, others at harvesting wild plants. Together they could put a meal together.

Furthermore, specialization was passed down via apprenticeships. When a young boy was ready to join the hunt and needed to learn how to throw a spear, he no doubt was attracted to the best spear thrower to teach him. If a young woman wanted to become a healer, she would apprentice to the clan's medicine woman.

Division of labor not only allowed the tribe to innovate faster, but it also created *dependency* on each other. The hunting party was successful only if the tip of the spear was sharp—they were all dependent on the "wood selecting specialist." Recall that being perceived by your mate as dependable makes you more attractive, and others depend on each specialist, another example of how tightly woven your instincts for success are.

You can *enhance cooperative effort between people by increasing their awareness that they are dependent on each other.* Social psychologists have discovered that when an individual feels others are depending on her to act in an expected manner (cooperatively), she is more likely to do the expected behavior.

Consider the coach who's giving a pep talk before the final playoff game. "Everybody is part of the team and everybody has to do their job for the team to win." True, yes, but not as powerful as the winning coach who emphasizes the *dependency between the players* and reminds them of their *personal responsibility to each other* to support each other during the game. Building teamwork by emphasizing that each player is dependent *on each other* for success, not dependent on the more abstract "team," is a smart play.

A project manager is wise to clarify in a team meeting the expectations and responsibilities for each participant, but wiser still is opening up the discussion so the team members interact with each other to personally reiterate and describe the roles and responsibilities they are to exchange with each other.

I'd be willing to bet that when a division of labor is absent or out of balance in your household, stress is paramount. It's a safe bet since it is true for your body. A family meeting in which everyone hears each other's household responsibilities is much more effective than individually nagging each other to get the chores done.

Learn to *leverage dependency in your communications.* "How many times have I told you to bring down your laundry?" or "You never help—bring down your laundry. I can't do everything." These phrases don't get the results: Mother and daughter work together to get the laundry done. The mother who knows how to co-op by creating a division of labor with her 16-year-old daughter says, "I can only wash your clothes if you have your laundry downstairs before dinner." She is *leveraging dependency* by implying "Doing your laundry is dependent on you getting it to me. You do your job; I'll do mine."

A division of labor also stimulates cooperation by creating *group win, with individual benefits*. The whole is greater than the sum of its parts. A win-win outcome is the beauty of the division of labor. Each cell or individual exchanges needed services with another, and even if each cell or individual is motivated by self-interest, the exchange is still beneficial to both.

You can boost cooperation by pointing out that *each person is better off cooperating than running solo*. "You might not like doing it, but you are better off if you do," is a message to hone to your situations. Accordingly, in the laundry scenario, the observant father would reinforce to his daughter what his wife said: "Sweetheart, I know it's a pain for you, but at least if you remember to take your clothes to the laundry room, you won't have to wash them yourself."

Emphasizing Identity

Thousands of students go their separate ways all week, but let them meet all together in college's "Big House," on a Saturday afternoon and they instantly become a pack of vicious wolverines eager to attack and rip to shreds the day's enemy. They unite for the victory of their pack.

Everything in life has an individual identity—animal, mineral, vegetable. Even the first particles of matter had an identity defined by their molecular properties. When we unite with others, we create a new identity, as when a man and woman marry and create a *couple identity*.

Many times, such as when going to college or taking a position with a new employer, you significantly modify your sense of self. A star athlete on one team who jumps to another team, which the year before he saw as his "enemy," assumes a new loyalty and identity. A computer salesman leaving his firm to join a competitor is doing the same, as is the college student who transfers from a Big Ten University to one in the PAC 10 tribe.

Such a change in identity often has psychological repercussions. It is human nature to be protective of your identity; first because it is defines you, and second because, as you recall, you are hardwired to be *loss averse*. We want to keep what we have. Consider that when people feel they've lost their identity, they frequently become depressed, and then are reinvigorated when they feel they have "reclaimed their identity" or "found themselves" with a new purpose. After a divorce, it's a given that both will experience sadness. They're mourning the loss of their marriage identity.

For your ancestors, identity as a mechanism for stimulating cooperation came into play when humans began to pair up (like molecules) into small groups of individuals. These small groups coagulated with others to form larger groups, reaching approximately 150 people, just about the critical mass with which your neo-cortex is comfortable in relating to at a social affair today.

As the stability of the relationships developed, because of a division of labor and reciprocity, a tribe emerged, a group of people living together, all playing by the same rules and united in the same rituals, values, and shared history—their tribal identity.

Each tribe evolved a differentiated identity and proudly proclaimed it in vibrant tattoos and face painting. Is this any different from sports team jackets, college sweatshirts, or polo shirts embroidered with the company logo? I think not.

As individuals continued getting their needs met by the community, it is easy to see how a need to belong came into being, and with it, a sense of being committed to the community. It would be maladaptive to drop out of the group, since exile equated with death. "I need to belong" formed into a fundamental instinct.

Yet, there is no free lunch. The price for being a member of the group was committing to performing their specialized contribution, cooperating, and reciprocating. You give to the group; you get the benefits of the group. Consider that group health insurance today is much cheaper than individual insurance, which is a big reason people stay in dead-end jobs—for the "benefits," not only the wages.

Because the community was empowering, individuals became more and more devoted to keeping it afloat, and the sense of pride in the group began. *Emphasizing the pride of identity cultivates cooperation.*

Of course, tribes did splinter and divide. And if the individual or group of individuals who left were top "specialists," their departure could be devastating, much like the top three software designers leaving a corporation to create their own startup. Retention of talent was key to survival.

The answer to this problem became *identity enhancement*—creating a prominent role for the individual, accompanied by perhaps a title, a tattoo, an article of clothing, or a "badge of honor." Today, identity enhancement can be a title, a bonus, a corner office, or special perks—corporate behaviors designed to keep the individual committed to the company.

A ton of research, especially from the field of social psychology but also in economics, confirms what Mother Nature has shown about the nature of identity and how it stimulates cooperation. For now, three points are relevant.

First, people become motivated to act cooperatively if there is *a fear or anxiety of identity loss that will lose benefits.* Many women, for example, "cooperate" in their marriage because, if they divorce, they will lose the identity status their marriage affords them. A troublesome employee often becomes cooperative, at least in the short term, if the employee thinks he will get fired otherwise. A slacking student might study harder for finals if she thinks failing is going to get her kicked out of school. Thus, *emphasizing identity loss* can be used to stimulate cooperation, especially when the identity is positive.

"You are in one of the finest business schools in the country. It will be a shame if you don't get the grades and can't say you graduated," is much more likely to spark the student to "cooperate" with professors than, "You'd better improve your grades," or, "You need to study more." The former statement emphasizes a loss of a current positive identity; the latter is just a vague ineffective motivational comment.

A project manager might tell her uncooperative team, "We will be disgraced if we can't meet the deadline." Few people want to be disgraced, so even the free rider ends up working hard.

A second point to note: Cooperation in an individual or a group can be stimulated by *enhancing the identity of the individual in the group or enhancing the general identity of the group.* Employee commitment to achieve group goals increases when the individual's status within the group is enhanced. Captains usually try the hardest. And, too, companies that give recognition to the groups within their organization are on the right track. Project teams that name themselves promote group pride. Universities that have pep rallies before every game are on track, too.

The third point: Identity can also stimulate cooperation if, in the absence of immediate payback, *it is perceived that acting cooperatively will pay off in the near future.* The father might say to his bright but lazy son, "It will be great if you are able to say you are a Wharton graduate." This statement does not emphasize identity loss; in contrast it emphasizes a *positive identity outcome*—being able to say, "I graduated from a premiere business school." Chances are likely the student will step it up, not because good grades are important to him, but because the resulting identity is positive and useful for future success. The lesson for a project manager is to let his team know how well they will be regarded if their project is successful.

All these points capitalize on your evolutionary heritage of being loss averse, so you are taking advantage of human hardwiring by using the threat of identity loss to motivate cooperation.

What about your marriage and family? Those who *stick together and enjoy each other* have a strong sense of identity, and each frequently enhances the identity of the other. Take the family photo holiday card. It's one way to emphasize family and couple identity; it's a proclamation to everybody: "We are happy to be together." Family meals and vacations are another way for everybody to experience family identity. Take a quick look at the walls in your home. Do you see family pictures? Are there pictures of you and your partner? Photo albums abound in families and marriages with a solid identity, and it's highly correlated with happiness.

Play Fair

Imagine your ancestors out on a hunt. Each agrees to stay at a strategic point to help ambush the big prey. The cooperative game is in the works. The wait is long, and at various times all four hunters are presented with individual opportunities to catch smaller prey that would be ample for at least themselves and their family, but to do so they would have to jeopardize the team project by abandoning their position—they would have to defect from the rules of the game.

Two of the hunters decide to "cheat," and when the big game comes stomping through, the honest hunters are left to do a job that requires more than two. Their honesty and commitment to the rules reaps them nothing. What happens the next time? One scenario is, since there is no reason to be honest and to act by the rules, that all the hunters desert their posts, and inevitably, all desert each other. A more probable one is that the two honest hunters will continue to work with each other, but not with the cheats.

From an evolutionary perspective, fairness evolved as a mechanism to keep the group going, to keep people in the game, to stimulate cooperation. As long as the rules are fair, there are few quitters. *Fairness is part of our nature.*

Studies support the notion that while you may be able to fool Mother Nature, you can't cheat her. The famous Wasson test is a psychological puzzle in which the individual is given four cards, face down. The instructions are to solve a puzzle by turning over as few cards as possible to prove a conditional statement, an *If-then rule*. Individuals do poorly when the dilemma is abstract and do well when it's precise and concrete.

Psychologists have determined the puzzle is easiest to solve when it is presented as some form of a social contract that needs to be policed or monitored to make sure rules are followed. In this format, even if the contract is deeply foreign and the social context unfamiliar, it becomes easier to solve. The interpretation of this finding is that we are hardwired to identify cheats.

Natural selection would favor those with this adaptation because it would allow individuals to be selective in deciding which people they want to deal with. To be able to "read" exploitive people is a huge advantage—you'll avoid engaging with them, a skill that even today saves you a lot of money and anguish.

Unfair, exploitive interactions fall apart fast. Fair people eventually push those who ignore the rules out of the game. Dealing only with fair people keeps business flourishing and keeps you in the game. If we had evolved as a species of cheaters, it would be impossible to form long-term relationships, intimate or business. There would be no good will, no trust, and, consequently, no cooperation. It would be a world that is hard to imagine because it probably could not exist. Human history indicates that societies where cheating and a lack of fairness were the norm are societies that inevitably crumbled. Corrupt societies today are those you flee from to find a better life.

Recognize the fact: The world detests cheaters. Whether it is on Wall Street or on a baseball field, cheaters typically are driven out of a group. It pays to play fair simply for the reason that it keeps you in the game.

What would be the evolved qualities of fairness that would keep a tribe and then a community stable? Based on what we know today, it would be qualities that comprise *procedural fairness*.

Procedural fairness is defined by two goals. The first is aimed at outcome—the punishment or the reward is perceived by the group as being contextually appropriate. A harsh punishment for a small infraction or an extravagant reward in relation to average performance would not meet the criterion, which is why disproportional acts typically provoke anger, a cue that something is wrong, injustice in this case. And talent is quick to abandon ship when it perceives it is not fairly compensated with money and recognition.

The second goal of procedural fairness is relationship-oriented: to ensure that that the same rules apply to everyone equally. Note that when we see exceptions to these rules—a celebrity walks from a DUI or the boss's son is not disciplined for coming to work late. We get angry at the injustice.

Count on the fact that communities in which members have equal *voice*, equal input on group decisions, were stimulating cooperation. Voice, or having a say, gives people a sense of control, and also a feeling that they are respected and accepted as an equal. These feelings motivate an individual to be part of a group, to cooperate and to contribute their best.

Managers will have more cooperative employees if they allow and encourage the employee to have their say in their performance appraisals—a true interaction. Letting your teenagers have voice in setting their curfew will increase their cooperation with family rules. Most parents arbitrarily set one.

In addition, *receiving fair treatment* would stimulate cooperation because it would promote Tit-Tit-Tit for Tat behavior. Because you expect equitable payback, you continue your good work on the assumption of fairness. Good work is rewarded appropriately. Those in the work force should know that broken promises pave the way to strikes, slowdowns, bad morale, and expensive turnover.

Parents are warned to make sure their kids *believe* that their reward promises will be delivered if they are to keep their kids cooperating, whether it is doing their division of labor, in the house, or their division of labor in school, their homework.

Fairness also fosters cooperation because it creates a sense of group/team/family belonging. One way people decide whether they have received fair treatment by the group is by comparing themselves to others in the group. When equality is perceived, members tend to treat each other as equals, and cooperation is stimulated. A sense of wanting to be part of the group emerges, to be one among equals.

Teachers who want their students to cooperate in the learning process should be vigilant in ensuring that every student has an equal opportunity to answer questions, lead projects, and be first in the lunch line. In other words, no "teacher's pets!"

Leadership advice: Stimulate the cooperation of your organization by making sure the troops *perceive* and *feel* they are treated *fairly.*

18

Co-Op Today

Reciprocity, division of labor, identity, and fairness are four inter-related tools that Mother Nature has evolved in us so that each of us can enhance our specialized skills through cooperation—working with others for the common good.

Here are some examples of how to co-op in different situations, several of which I am sure will resonate with you, and some sugges-tions that might surprise you. Also, keep in mind that if you are in the midst of any of them, and if *what you are doing is not working*—your solution might be using the genius of your instincts.

Commit to Cooperate

For *you* to immediately reap the benefits of *your* cooperative instincts, *commit to cooperate*. You achieve this by accepting the fact that you will often have to play Tit, Tit, Tit, Tat. Simply stated, be will-ing to do more than your fair share to foster cooperative relation-ships, with your partner, with your kids, and with your colleagues. You already know the end game. Your persistent efforts to cooperate inevitably trigger greater reciprocity and more cooperative play—a benefit to you, and your Selfish Jean.

Managing your emotions is essential. Anger and resentment toward others—such as hoarding grudges—will sabotage your positive instinct to cooperate. You will end up playing Tit for Tat, eventually a losing scenario in game rooms and real life. Buffer these emotions by remembering *you* reap the benefits of cooperation—hello, Selfish Jean.

Note: You can always sit down with an individual and explain that you need a more cooperative effort, but set the tone and set an example by increasing *your own* efforts to stimulate the cooperative efforts of others. On this point, Mother Nature's slogan would be, "Just Commit!"

Interdepartmental Conflict

Interdepartmental conflict is a frequent topic in my executive classes. Dozens of times I've heard the comments that describe the scenario:

- "The departments are at war with each other."
- "They never meet the deadlines."
- "Nobody talks to each other."
- "They are very competitive with us."
- "They withhold information."

The list goes on and on, all ending with the same result: Two departments are not working together for the good of the company.

In business seminars, the most common suggestion is for each department to raise the issue with their respective leader and let the two leaders work things out. Sorry to say, this is rarely effective, as the class admits. Going to the noncooperative individual's manager proves to be an equally ineffective maneuver. So what do you do? How would you stimulate cooperation? What would Mother Nature recommend?

I'll give you some clues. The first is that reciprocity is the tool to stimulate. The second is that I typically hear this from people operating in *large* organizations, mostly Fortune 500 companies. Third is about the size of your ancestral tribes and your communities. Combine the three and you come up with a solution for enhancing interdepartmental cooperation; it's called the *interdepartmental intermingle.*

The interdepartmental intermingle draws its power from the reciprocity point—recognition. People have to know you to cooperate with you. Your ancestral communities and tribes reached no more than 150 people, the approximate number of people/relationships that your social brain is equipped to handle today. It's been my observation that in large organizations, when interdepartmental conflict occurs, most people are not even familiar with those in the other department. Their communications are delivered through emails, internal memos, or a brief phone exchange—exactly the opposite of your human nature, since you've been hardwired for face-to-face communication.

Your evolutionary heritage advises a strategy that allows people to know each other on a more personal level, to deepen the recognition with each other, so when an extra cooperative effort is needed, reciprocity recognition will achieve it. Is it any wonder that top salespeople consistently meet their clients face-to-face, even when it requires expensive travel? "Face time" builds familiarity and trust—naturally, the face communicates.

Thus, department heads who need to maximize interdepartmental cooperation are wise to launch a preemptive strike an intermingle, a positive event that brings together people from *both* or multiple departments.

While it is common practice to have a big department get-together, most large companies will vouch that it is rare that there are large interdepartmental gatherings. Throw in a short talk, if you will, but the major focus should be social and casual, to allow individuals to become familiar with each other on a personal level. Letting employees get to know a bit about the others' personal interests and families fosters trust on a deeper level than talking about work. "It's personal, not business," would be Mother Nature's tag line for thwarting interdepartmental conflict.

Reducing Marital Conflict

Reducing marital conflict would be a sweeps week topic for afternoon talk shows, and there would be no better guest expert than Mother Nature. What would she tell viewers whose marriages are going cold and crumbling, and are filled with contentious conversations? In two words: *reenergize reciprocity*.

Consider that our closest relatives are chimpanzees. Primatologists who study chimps observe that male chimps exchange meat with females for sex. Anthropologists have found the same patterns in human tribes—male hunters exchange meat with females for sex. In tribes where men are gone for weeks at a time on hunting expeditions, promiscuity among both sexes is rampant, whereas in tribes where meat is plentiful and hunts are brief, monogamy is the rule. So, it is a fair assumption that early, early prototypes of current man also exchanged meat for sex. You can see how men would benefit from this exchange—the more sexual partners, the greater the chance for more offspring to carry on his genes. The female, for her part, received doses of protein that would ensure her own genes were passed on to healthier children.

However, a big difference between chimps and humans is the institution of marriage, a universal institution in our species. Whereas chimps lose interest in the females, humans enter into long-term bonds, often for life. This enduring bond introduces an underlying feature of marriage—*long-term reciprocity*, a long-term give and take that is mutually beneficial.

While the man would still continue to hunt for meat to share with his woman and children, he would now get to share the nutrients from the vegetables and fruits that his partner gathered and enjoy the comfortable home she created. Because of what they both brought to the table, each was better off. Reciprocity has been part of marriage ever since. Furthermore, the long-term relationship boosts the reciprocity "stakes." Now that the man was still providing sustenance to his partner, he would also come to expect that she take care of his off-spring as her contribution. Perhaps this is a primal reason why so many men get angry when their wives are "not taking care of the kids."

Marriage is an exchange, a contract in which both partners pledge to continue their long-term reciprocity, for better or for worse. When it's an unbalanced equation, it's for the worse.

I've found, and I believe most therapists would agree, that when conflict dominates a marriage, or when one partner feels short-changed or taken for granted, it often stems from a lack of reciprocity or a change in the nature of the reciprocity.

How is the reciprocity in your marriage? What do you bring to the table? Does your partner think it is "fair," or even something he needs? Your ancestors needed meat and fruit. The truth is, what you contributed in the early years of your marriage might not be what your partner needs today.

You might feel a bit awkward, or anxious, but asking your partner what she feels you bring to the table will start to clarify whether reciprocity is working for or against you. If against, you know what you need to do: Reenergize your reciprocity. This means you make your end of the exchange equation more appealing to your partner, perhaps by adding more of what is good, or adding new factors into your half of the exchange equation that sweeten the deal, such as a willingness to travel more.

Your success depends on your ability to avoid falling into the trap: "I'll only do my share if you do yours." Mother Nature says you will enjoy your marriage more if you remember that your Tit-Tit-Tit (give-give-give) play will bring out the same in your partner. It's also important to get your partner to recognize what you do bring to the table. Of course, this does not mean you do it in a Tit for Tat manner or guilt-ridden way, or by shaming and blaming, but getting your partner to realize your contributions to the relationship is usually helpful in reducing marital conflict.

One couple, for example, changed the *conversational nature* of their reciprocity. They found that much of their daily conversations focused on the obligations of marriage—their kids, chores, bills—hardly the stuff that energizes relationships. They remembered that when they fell in love, they talked for hours about ideas, books, movies, and politics. They agreed that on "date night" they would ban all talk of obligations, to rekindle their love for each other and create time and space for them to be themselves, not just parents.

Creating Coworker Cooperation

In a presentation titled "The Nature of Cooperation," I made the point that you can stimulate cooperation between people by engaging them in tasks that *require them to cooperate*, rather than simply discussing how they can work together more cooperatively.

A few weeks later, a manager who listened well phoned me to tell me how he cunningly used this strategy. Two of his key staff members were entrenched in open power struggles. Their bad blood was creating costly project delays.

He told me he took both of them to lunch, intentionally choosing a Chinese restaurant. Before the waiter took their order, he subtly remarked, "Well, I like everything. You two decide what to order." This prompted a short discussion, and they agreed on which dishes to select. During the meal, they handed the platters around the table, and the manager kept the conversation focused on the ingredients and tastes of the dishes. After all was happily consumed, the manager said, "You guys did a good job in ordering; everything went well together. And when we get back to the office, I will expect the two of you to cooperate in the same manner." To cement his point, he let them split the check.

Co-op (co-operation) took form in this example, by getting each "hostile army" to sit down together to break bread. He forced them to cooperate by stimulating a division of labor (each had to propose dishes) and fairness (they both had to like or be willing to try a particular dish) and then used it to point out to them that they were capable of cooperating with each other for the common good, exactly what was required when they returned to the office. And so they did.

Apply this strategy in your own marriage. A ballroom dance class will force you to coordinate your efforts to a common goal, whereas going to a movie requires you to sit silently next to each other, engaged in the film instead of each other. You are much better off to have danced all night.

Do activities with your kids that require parent-child cooperation. Pitch a tent together, set up a badminton net, build a tree fort, or go for a canoe trip on the river. These activities require interaction and mutual effort.

Sibling Rivalry to Sibling Support

It is a nightmarish reality for many parents—your children constantly squabble and compete over everything, including your attention and affection.

Sibling rivalry—the familiar term describes continual competition between your children, and most psychologists will tell you that if it is not managed effectively, it can follow them into their adult years.

Most parents attempt to manage the situation by being "fair" to each child. This is always destined for failure because sooner or later, circumstances arise that cause one child to scream, "That's not fair!" All parents know the inevitability of violating the "Treat your kids equally" doctrine.

Mother Nature would handle the sibling rivalry between her children differently. Her goal is not to treat each child with equality, but rather, to *turn the competitive nature of the children's relationship into a cooperative and supportive one.*

How might you co-op fairness between your children? One skill-teaching strategy would be to play games that emphasize taking turns and following the rules. It is *how* you play the game that counts, in the end.

Along these lines, stimulate cooperation by changing the rules of a competitive game into a cooperative task. Ping-Pong and tennis, for example, become a cooperative experience when the task is to see how long you can keep a rally going. When I was growing up, my next-door neighbor and I had a Ping-Pong rally in which the ball went over the net at least 1,000 times. In a win/lose game, our longest volley would be ten times. In retrospect, the longer rally was much more *fun* than winning. It's the one I remember.

Assign co-op chores that can only be accomplished by their joint efforts—a clean room for a week, setting or clearing the family table, growing a vegetable garden. For "success," the children become dependent on each other. Mother Nature would predict you would find your kids encouraging each other and, over time, Tit-Tit-Tit (give, give, give) play emerges. You used the "prisoner's dilemma" game to your advantage!

Take advantage of their hardwiring for identity by creating a *sibling identity*, one that they want to share. Refer to it often; they will feel pride and want to act as a team. You may play a family game of scrabble: Mr. and Mrs. Baker against the "Fabulous Baker Boys." It works with any name. When you stimulate a positive sibling identity, you encourage your children to feel proud of each other and work as a team.

A caution from Mother Nature: Sadly, too many parents encourage competition between their children—"See if you can beat your brother"; "The one who gets straight A's gets to take four friends to the water park." The win/lose game does more harm than good. It results in lowered self-esteem in the loser. More damage is done by communicating there is an inequality between them. It sets in motion a lifelong course of trying to prove that they are as good as or better than each other. So familiar is this theme, you've probably seen it theatrically.

In effect, parents who encourage sibling competition are helping their children disconnect from their instincts to be cooperative and care giving to those who are biologically closest. Don't be one of these parents.

Cooperate to Compete

We rarely like to act like baboons but perhaps, at times, we should. A characteristic of baboons is that one male will frequently "steal" a female from another baboon. Even if the female belongs to a much stronger male, they have figured out how to successfully "kidnap" females. *They form coalitions and alliances.*

In action: Two small baboons desire a frisky female that belongs to a much stronger male. Individually, neither is strong enough to kidnap her, but together, they can overcome him. Of course, they will still have to compete against each other for her affections, but with the big baboon out of the way, they each have a chance at winning her.

Reflect on the example, and you realize that Mother Nature created an effective cooperative building strategy that often turns competition into cooperation: a common enemy. You've seen it hundreds of times: Two teams both rooting for a third to lose—a benefit to both, competing companies coordinating their resources to compete with larger organizations, children pooling their efforts to fool their common enemy—their parents, countries uniting to fight terrorism. All these coalitions have the common denominator of uniting competitors to win victory over a common adversary.

The key then to stimulate coalitions is *identifying "the bad guy,"* the common enemy that makes people want to cooperate, even if they are at odds with each other. The real enemy of the smaller franchise might not be each other but the 1,000-pound gorilla that is squeezing their market share. A coalition here is beneficial to both. The baseball team pitcher bickers every day with the catcher. The coach ends the warfare by continually emphasizing in his pregame pep talks: "The real enemy is the other team." A group of competitive students share their knowledge when they realize the real threat is the test, not their ranking in the scores.

You don't have to "sleep with the enemy." But the lesson here is to be on the watch for opportunities in which coalitions can help you succeed.

A derivation is *emphasizing the common goal*—from meeting the project deadline to winning the game. Common *positive and meaningful goals* unite people. They stimulate positive identity and wanting to be part of the group. Cooperative language is important here. Words such as "we," "our," "us," "our team," and "our family" emphasize the common goal: "*We're all* going to make this project successful"; "*Our plan* is really strong."

How about coalitions on a global level? For those of you up on international affairs, you know that two ancient allies and modern competitors are rebuilding their ties as their governments decided to fight poverty, not each other. Their cooperation is expected to lead to unparalleled economic growth for both.

Similarly, I remember a member of the Young Presidents Organization telling me about a program he funded at a prestigious East Coast university. He said: "Each year I bring two students from conflicting countries to the university. They room together, and their studies involve coming up with common problems and how they can solve them. They leave with a greater understanding of how cooperation can be a tool for their success." The same president also told me that he would often put people from warring countries in business deals together. "A lot of problems between people go away," he told me, "when people see how they can make money together," a common goal for most.

The Cooperative Culture

You already know some of the features of an effective corporate culture. Now, you can add cooperative to the list. Recall that there is an abundance of research indicating that cooperation, not competition, brings out the best in people. Think about the cooperative instincts and ways they could be played out in today's corporate world.

I can offer a fast four:

- First, implement *team performance appraisals*. Mother Nature would advocate this to stimulate cooperation via division of labor and positive identity.
- Second, cooperative cultures are *fair cultures*, so appropriate compensation and equality of treatment is mandatory.
- Third, *encourage socialization*—a big cafeteria to help people mingle; corporate-sponsored social clubs, bowling leagues, softball teams, and bus outings to theme parks and major art exhibitions are a few suggestions.
- Fourth, *corporate identity logos* and sayings everywhere will facilitate pride and participation.

To summarize the chapter: Your work, your family, your marriage—enhance them all by using your cooperative instincts.

Part VI

Curious?...So You Can Stay
Ahead of the Pack

Enhance your life by using your curiosity instincts

19

Accelerating Your Learning

Your Evolutionary Heritage

The chimpanzee is innately curious. Put him in a jungle or a room with dozens of objects, and he will touch, taste, shake, and investigate each one. His curiosity leads to learning about his environment and serendipitous learning.

The drive to explore and investigate the environment is universal across species. Curiosity is the impetus for scientific discovery—snooping on our neighbors, putting the man on the moon, and even being hooked on crossword puzzles. If you have ever stayed up late to watch the end of a movie only to be exhausted the next morning, or felt compelled to watch the end of a football game, you can blame it on curiosity, the instinct that bestows on us our drive to explore, investigate, comprehend, and master our world.

Curiosity is more powerful the higher you climb the evolutionary ladders. Philosophers call it a passion for learning, a thirst, a desire, or a need for knowledge, and they posit that a civilized culture can be measured by the hunger of its people for learning and adventure and the degree to which its great minds of the time are boldly speculative.

Consider what life would be like without the genius of this instinct. There would be no discovery of America, no vaccine for polio, and no computers. You would have no interests beyond primal drives of hunger and sex. For sure you would not be reading this book, because it would not have been written.

Your Curiosity Instinct

Curiosity as a life enhancer is best understood when we think about it in terms of its technical evolutionary function: focusing our attention and sparking movement toward an object to investigate whether it will advance our survival. A scene from a seminal film illustrates the components of curiosity, why we're hardwired to have it, and a few basics about how it works.

The title sequence begins with the image of the Earth rising over the moon while the sun rises over the Earth. Superimposed over wide shots of the African desert, a caption reads, "The Dawn of Man." A tribe of prehistoric ape men is struggling to survive in the parched desert. As the sun rises, the tribe is awakened by a compelling sound coming from a tall, black monolith that inexplicably has appeared during the night. The ape men are terrified but also excited. They approach warily, retreating now and then—their curiosity at war with their fear. Finally, the most "curious" reaches out his hand and touches the singing monolith. They return to camp, and the ape man who stroked the ebony surface invents the first tool. He picks up a bone from a pile and starts clubbing the other bones to crush them. Now he's standing almost upright, and he leads his clan in defense of their waterhole. He clubs an enemy ape man with his newfound weapon. Victorious, he spins his bone club high in the air. As it falls downward, it turns into an orbiting satellite.

Even if this isn't the most accurate telling of the Dawn of Man, it illustrates the key components of curiosity and how it is the engine that drives evolution.

Nature's Energy

Hardwired into your brain's reticular formation and hypothalamus is Mother Nature's power source, the innate energy, the raw motivational essence that is instilled into every organism. Without arousal there is no movement. If the ape men were not aroused, they would not have the energy to explore the monolith. Similarly, if your child is not aroused by his homework, there will be no effort to do it. Arousal is a requisite for action—mental and physical.

Because curiosity is the instigator of exploratory and investigative behaviors, it follows that curiosity mediates arousal by giving it direction. In other words, curiosity is the selection process that guides our perception and attention and, thus, keeps our brain from treating with equal importance the multitude of stimuli that bombard our sensory receptors at all times.

Some things arouse our curiosity, and these are the things— whether a geographical location or a subject matter or a noise in our house—that we explore and investigate. A manager who wants to develop her staff's skills might be more effective in delegating assignments based on staff's curiosity rather than task competency. Doing the former, would cause motivation to *develop* the knowledge and skills to successfully complete the task.

Natural selection would favor those who used their curiosity adaptation because it motivated them to explore their environment for objects that could enhance their survival; ape men who did not touch the monolith did not enhance their intelligence. Just like today, the student or manager who is curious—motivated to quench his thirst for knowledge, typically finds school and managerial performance enhanced, to say nothing of the positive arousal feelings experienced by learning.

Curiosity also served your ancestors' survival because it drew their attention to objects or events that were threats. Imagine a group of your very early ancestors sitting around, when one's attention is aroused by a novel noise. His curiosity now directs his body movements to the source of the sound, and in so doing, allows his fellows to follow his movements so they all see the man-eating predator approaching and seek safety.

Stimulating arousal, then, is what gets curiosity in play, and when curiosity plays, you are motivated to explore and investigate. Mother Nature is telling you a point to remember: *Curiosity is the primary factor to stimulate for learning and for motivation.*

What arouses your curiosity? For openers, consider the properties of objects that draw your attention.

The Curious Object

An object that we respond to is called a stimulus. Your boss, partner, a package on your desk are all stimuli, each possessing specific attributes that send messages to your brain. Some of these messages arouse curiosity.

What is it about an object, a person, or a job that makes you curious? What causes you to explore? For the most part, it seems Mother Nature has hardwired us to respond to specific stimulus properties with curiosity. Not to get too far ahead of ourselves, but it is this evolutionary heritage that helps you artfully leverage these properties to stimulate curiosity in yourself and others.

The first curiosity stimuli is the *psychophysical* aspect—size, shape, color, sound, and symmetry. For the ape man, it could have been the height of the monolith, its color, its smoothness, and the sound that blended the voices of men and women singing with the sounds of birds and animals—the sound of life.

Ecological properties also arouse curiosity. The nature of these properties is that they are *affect-laden*—that is, associated with biological functions such as hunger, thirst, sex, and fear. With these properties in mind, you can again see how natural selection would favor those who used their curiosity adaptation. Curiosity aroused by the sight of the nubile cave woman would arouse sexual interest and begin the process of exploratory behavior for finding a mate, a prerequisite for increasing the chances that there will be offspring to carry on the genes. Stimuli that aroused hunger would direct your ancestors to possible food sources and thus would explain hunter-gathering behavior. If you have ever been at a large social affair, you have probably become curious about what is being served on the other side of the room; your curiosity arouses you to explore so that you might hunt and gather from the buffet.

The third set of stimuli is the most important in curiosity. We can call these properties *collative:* novelty, complexity, incongruity, and ambiguity. They evoke *feelings of uncertainty*, and uncertainty, more than anything else, stimulates human curiosity.

In the days of your ancestors, every object had elements of uncertainty, so every object was a curious object, and the abundance of them became a natural stimulant of curiosity, a motivator for hunting and gathering.

How Curiosity Works

The fundamental premise in living things is balance, the primal urge to remain in our *comfort zone*. All organisms have an optimal *physical arousal state*. It's pleasurable and reassuring. We're motivated to stay inside this zone, or seek an even more pleasurable zone. Rarely, do we try to make ourselves more stressed.

Curiosity causes a shift in the physiological arousal of the organism, which removes the organism from its arousal comfort zone. In an effort to return to its arousal comfort zone, the organism becomes motivated to explore its environment, to engage in *approach behavior*. It has become curious.

Curiosity arousal is pleasurable, backed by the research that confirms there are aversion and reward centers in your brain that receive messages, and those that stimulate curiosity are directed to reward centers. The monolith did not frighten or repel the ape man, it attracted him. Because curiosity arousal is pleasurable, the organism freely engages in *comfortably increasing investigative and exploratory* behavior and by doing so, increases the chances that it will encounter something that is life enhancing, be it reading a new book or meeting a new person.

When you can instigate exploratory behavior, you accelerate learning in yourself and others, which is the true value of curiosity.

20

Becoming a Curious George/Georgette

I have never met anyone who didn't love Curious George, the monkey. So besides accelerating your learning, being curious makes you more attractive. We like to be with curious people. We find them more interesting, more energetic, and more social.

Being curious also creates favorable impressions. As parents, we are happy to hear the teacher say, "You have an inquisitive child." And "openness to new ideas," is always a plus on a performance appraisal.

More important to many people, being curious enhances your bottom line. The sales rep who is curious about his clients is apt to discover new ways to serve them, thereby increasing his own wealth (hello, selfish genes), and is ahead of his less curious colleague. The engineer whose curiosity persists will be the one who invents the breakthrough technology, reaping the benefits that go with it. Being curious pays off, so it is no wonder Curious George is successful.

You, too, can become a Curious George/Georgette, but first, you have to stimulate your curiosity instincts on a daily basis. This means—and this is an everyday process for weeks and weeks—you need to *"Alpha up your arousal, regulate your arousal, stimulate intellectual curiosity, and behaviorally investigate."* Then you can put curiosity into play in all aspects of your life, whether it's to enhance your sex life, make a manager more effective, or create family fun.

Alpha Up Your Arousal

Natural selection has created differential levels of arousal. Some people are simply hardwired with more and are more easily stimulated to arousal than others. Some of us are inherently more curious, more motivated to learn and invent. While alpha dogs, for example, immediately investigate the objects in a room, the lazier dog pads to the corner to curl up and nap. Naturally, government agencies select only alpha dogs for search and rescue, drug-sniffing, and as guard dogs in airports.

Curiosity requires effort and energy, whether it is to take an atypical stroll in the park or to explore a new data bank for prospective clients. Thus, the first step in stimulating your curiosity instincts is to *Alpha up your energy level*. The goal is to have high energy on a daily basis, making it easier to act out your curiosity instinct. Often, people feel the urge to explore but are just too tired to make the effort.

When you Alpha up your arousal, you are practicing energizing yourself, and when you Alpha up your arousal daily, you have more energy to expend. In essence, you are self-motivating, which is exactly what curiosity does. It motivates you.

Mother Nature gives us some specifics on how we can increase our energy potential, all of which would be favored in natural selection.

The first is what you eat. Hunting took a lot of energy, so it is easy to see how natural selection would favor those who had high energy when big game appeared. Those who had the energy to run down the game were rewarded with the choice cuts—the original protein shake—and this, like today, gave them an energy boost. To eat for energy, not because of taste would be Mother Nature's eating strategy. Today, we can do both.

You already know that eating behavior is a big problem for most people, so give yourself some help. Perhaps a food energy chart in your kitchen will remind you of what your protein, carb, fruit, and vegetable intake should be. Customize your plan by consulting your physician or diet guru. It directly impacts your energy level. If you can't do it by yourself, care solicit for the support you need.

Now that you've upped your physical energy, you can boost it even more with *positive self-talk*, internal cognitive motivation. The power of positive thinking has been confirmed by countless clinical studies. You've heard the stories of winning athletes and people who overcame enormous adversity. "It's a mental game"; "I never gave up"; "I just kept telling myself to keep going, I could do it" are the typical phrases, even the little red engine told itself the same.

It's easy to see how natural selection favored those who developed the trait of generating positive, self-motivating thoughts. Hunting and gathering could be difficult, often resulting in perilous situations. Early humans, whose internal speech urged them on, increased their chances to survive because their *self-statements* increased their level of arousal to be used for motivational energy. Naturally, these positive thinkers would go on to achieve stronger ecological niches, just like today.

Today's research in cognitive psychology consistently confirms that a person's self-statements are a major mediator in regulating their physical arousal. You can either increase or decrease your level of physiological arousal by how you speak to yourself. Thus, like many of your ancestors, you can use self-statements as "mental steroids" to juice yourself up.

Jot down a few motivational phrases and make them highly visible in your home and office, even your car. It might sound hokey but, the fact is, plenty of data shows that the chances are good you will inevitably habituate these statements into your everyday thinking. The payoff is more energy and motivation.

Conversely, it's easy to see how natural selection rules against humans whose internal thoughts told them to quit, that they could not make it over the hill. Far from motivational, these thoughts sapped their energy, the power source for motivation. Consequently, they could not muster up what was needed to secure a strong ecological niche.

Moreover, consider the research on depression. The *depression triad* is

- Negative thoughts about oneself
- Negative thoughts about the current moment
- Negative thoughts about the future

Early humans whose thoughts went in this direction doomed themselves. Furthermore, since hereditary factors are at play in depression, is it so unreasonable to think that for some of us, the depression triad has been hardwired into our thinking? One common prescription to counteract the low energy caused by depression is to get at least an hour a day of moderate cardio exercise—walking, dancing, biking. It boosts our oxygen intake and energizes all our cells.

A third way to Alpha up is by taking advantage of one of the psychophysical stimuli properties that arouse your curiosity: sound. Recall that the ape man was aroused by the siren song of the monolith. Why would sound arouse us?

The evolutionary answer is that sound carries and communicates information and emotion. Animals can't talk, but their growls and purrs serve the same function. Wolves have a range of approximately 22 howls. Some communicate that a hunt is to start, while another communicates a call for help. In humans, our basic communication vocalizations are instinctual. No one had to teach you to make sounds of anger or whimper when you are hurt, and most mothers are almost 100 percent accurate in differentiating a baby's cry to be changed versus the cry to be picked up and held.

Sound arouses emotion, so the key here is to use sound to arouse you. One type of sound that can do this is music. Most people have a favorite song or two that psyches them up, be it the theme song from their favorite movie or a pop tune. The strategy here is to listen to the music that energizes you, whether it is when you wake up, are on the way to work, or the background music at your store that motivates customers to feel good so they'll buy your products. Music is used pervasively to impact your arousal, whether it's the organ at a sporting event or the music in a supermarket. Music gives you energy, sometimes enough to dance.

It is hard to be a curious George if you don't have daily energy, so Alpha up!

Overcoming Your Aversion Instinct

Call to mind the evolutionary function of curiosity. It directs your attention and behavior to objects that may enhance your survival. At the same time, the object of your curiosity could be hazardous. Thus, the ape man approaches the novel object before him with caution—his behavior looks like dancing—two steps forward, one step back, two forward; the dance repeated until he is close enough to touch it.

While curiosity motivates the forward movement, what is it that causes the ape man to almost simultaneously back off, like the student who backs off from an interesting assignment or an employee who avoids the task, despite interest in it?

The best answer is our *aversion instinct*—experienced as arousal discomfort and associated with anxiety and fear.

You are hardwired with arousal, and it is also true that you are hardwired with different types of arousal. While *curiosity arousal* to approach is pleasurable, *anxiety/fear arousal* is distressful; these distressful messages are sent to the brain's aversion center and instigate avoidance behavior—in the name of survival, but at the cost of exploring.

Many times, these conflicting messages fire simultaneously, and when avoidance dominates, curiosity is inhibited. For example, novelty is a stimulus property that arouses curiosity. Yet, if the

object or situation is *too* novel, avoidance—the feeling of anxiety—
is triggered.

A student might be curious about a particular college, but as
soon as he gets the phone-book-size course catalogue in the mail
and reads the theoretical course descriptions, his curiosity is
attacked by anxiety. It is not that he's no longer interested in the
school; it's that he's overwhelmed. To the parent's dismay, "He's lost
interest." But Mother Nature would say, "He's still interested. *Help
him manage his avoidance arousal* so he does not retreat prema-
turely so he can see if the school is of real interest." On the same
point, it is true that many people initially start a job training task
with high curiosity and motivation to learn, but the initial complexity
and size of the task creates avoidance arousal; it overcomes their
energy and motivation.

It is this aversion response fueled by arousal discomfort that dis-
connects us from using our curiosity instinct, whether it is in the context of a child asking a question, or a couple who want to learn more
about each other sexually.

Thus, to *follow through* on the curiosity you stimulate in yourself
and others, you have to be tuned in to the fact that you have to minimize the discomfort arousal that prevents exploration, be it an assignment, a job, or another person.

Regulating Arousal

The ape man's cautious approach to the monolith shows us the
winning maneuver: Approach the new using small steps. First, *small
steps allow you to get comfortable in the increase of arousal that
accompanies exploratory types of behavior.* Indeed, for the past 100
years, psychology has accepted the theory that small, incremental

changes in physical arousal are perceived as being pleasurable, while large or sudden changes are deemed distressing. When you think and act in small steps forward, you find it easier to manage the anxiety and fear that often go hand-in-hand with starting something new. Mothers who teach their children to swim by slowly easing them into the water, step by step, are capitalizing on this point, as is the teacher who breaks down a complex assignment into small assignments.

The second benefit of taking small steps is that it allows you to engage in *longer periods* of exploratory and investigative behavior. It enables you to explore in depth. Think about the last time you started a new hobby, skill, or relationship, and what caused you to retreat or quit. Was it because you moved too fast and got overwhelmed?

You can see how taking it slowly would be helpful to your ancestors. It allowed them to overcome their fears, so they could continue their exploratory activities and thus improve their chances for finding new pieces of their environment that could be survival-friendly. Those who developed an interest in what makes people sick enhanced all of our health, and the same could be said of your ancestors who developed an interest in understanding what makes meat rotten. It allowed them to learn about cause and effect, invent tools and tactics, and gain advanced knowledge.

Contemporary psychology has discovered other means for you to learn how to regulate your arousal, such as relaxation, yoga, meditation, and self-statements. These are all effective and require practice.

Consider, though, that taking things in small steps as a way to regulate your arousal is not only Mother Nature's advice for keeping your curiosity high—and, thus, motivation up—but is also easy to do because you don't need to practice or do anything new—just the opposite: Act like the ape man.

Significantly, the simultaneous arousal of curiosity and avoidance is a Mother Nature mechanism that helps us proceed with caution. This being the case, "Throw caution to the wind" is not good advice. Yet "reckless" people continually do it, usually with calamitous results.

Stimulating Intellectual Curiosity

There are different types of curiosity. You have seen one kind when you observe an animal sniffing at a new object it encounters. Another type of curiosity is historically referred to as a scientific curiosity and metaphysical wonder. This type of curiosity generates a different brand of arousal, one that motivates the quest for knowledge, a curiosity that is not satisfied until it finds what it needs to know. This is the *intellectual curiosity* that is the basis for motivation to learn and discover and leads to one's own enhancement and to the enhancement of others. Intellectual curiosity is needed to develop interests and, more broadly, to accelerate your learning. In fact, disconnection from intellectual curiosity is one of the traits that characterize people as disinterested, nonmotivated, and inefficient (because their lack of intellectual curiosity prevents them from developing themselves and learning new ways to handle the tasks they encounter).

How do you stimulate this type of intellectual curiosity? The first thing to know is that it is aroused by *collative properties*, particularly information gaps in knowledge, conflicting concepts, or missing data in the scientific world. The brain responds to an inconsistency or a gap in its knowledge, just as the musical brain responds to a dissonant chord.

Information gaps and conceptual conflicts arouse discomfort, so the intellectual curiosity goes into action to return to a sense of balance and our comfort zone. A scientist who is relentless in her pursuit of identifying the cause of a problem exemplifies intellectual curiosity, as was your ancestral explorer who felt compelled to sail into uncharted seas. They *have to know the answers*, and they *feel restless and dissatisfied* until they do.

A good way to stimulate your intellectual curiosity so you can enjoy the pleasures and benefits it provides is to create "information gaps" within yourself. You will have to "get down and experiential" and learn some intellectual curiosity exercises. A considerable amount of research indicates that you can increase your intellectual curiosity, and thus enhance your life, by discovering new interests, skills, and information. I'll start you with two novel curiosity tasks, both for the purpose of helping you stimulate your motivation to learn.

First, select what you think is the most interesting appliance in your house—a DVD player, microwave, television, or iPod are some of the common choices. Now, stimulate your intellectual curiosity by creating an information gap—ask yourself, "How does it work?" and use this information gap to arouse yourself to discover the answer so you can explain it. If that's beyond you, start by discovering the cause and effect relationship that satisfies the curiosity of the five-year-old's question: "Why is the sky blue?" The point here is to *experience the pleasure of satisfying curiosity arousal through learning*.

When you repeatedly experience the pleasure of learning, you become internally motivated, and this is when learning is fun. You want to learn for the sake of learning, and your curiosity stays alive. By the way, don't be surprised if after you can explain one appliance, your curiosity directs you to another.

It is also an intellectual curiosity stimulant to engage in a 15-minute nightly Self-Socratic-like dialogue. Like Socrates in ancient Greece, ask yourself a question, and no matter how you answer, question your answer. Make it a complex philosophical question. Complexity, remember, is the stimulant of intellectual curiosity.

Persistent self-questioning and exploring your answers helps you increase *your tolerance for a higher curiosity arousal level—* your ability to stay in novel and complex situations that might have overwhelmed you in the past. Your increased comfort with confronting the novelty, complexity, and uncertainty of a situation allows you to explore and investigate more fully, be it a person or a job assignment. You develop *intellectual staying power*; the student can now get through the first 50 pages and then can enjoy the rest of the book.

Natural selection favored those who engaged in such a practice because it fostered mental skills such as analyzing cause and effect and inventing new tools. Ancestors who became curious about the relationship of weather to gardening, I am sure, ended up in a bed of roses compared to those who never thought about cause and effect.

Continually experiencing the *pleasure of learning* and *increasing your intellectual staying power* makes it a lot easier to engage in the final requisite for intellectual curiosity.

Act Curiously

"Act curiously" is just another way of saying, "explore and investigate." These behaviors bring your curiosity instincts to life. One way is to engage in novel and fun activities. Novelty arouses, and fun makes arousal changes pleasurable. Together, these factors make it easier for you to get out of your comfort zone and explore and create.

Instead of going to the same restaurant, read some reviews and select one you've never been to before, in a neighborhood or nearby town you've never explored. Mix up your routine. Instead of your weekly golf or tennis game with the same people, try something new: a museum, a park, or an ethnic community where you can shop and have lunch in a "foreign" environment. Do whatever you think is fun and whatever you haven't done before.

Start an activity that you have always been curious to try—a "Dancing with the Stars" ballroom dance class, perhaps. And do your homework first; don't just jump in. Take small steps. Your first acting curious behavior might simply be to gather some information about availability, location, and fees. If you are still interested, your curiosity will motivate you to learn more—such as the types of classes, the music played, and so on until you are curious enough to sign up.

Act out your intellectual curiosity by taking advantage of your increasing intellectual staying power. Do this by setting up a *time lock*—a specific time of your day that you will read any article in any magazine or newspaper that *interests* you. Do it every day for a month, and it will be self-motivating because you are hardwired to enjoy the development of your interests and learning. As you do this more often, you will become more and more curious, and more motivated to learn and discover the world around you.

The four steps I have outlined to stimulate your curiosity instincts need to be thought of as *daily activities* to integrate into your life. The repetitiveness of performing them will make them a skill and habit, a tool that will reward you in enthusiasm, more developed interests, positive self-esteem, and a host of other positives.

In spirit, Mother Nature's final point here is: Be curious; you'll like it!

21

Curiosity Every Day

The genius of your curiosity instinct is that it inspires imagination, confidence, and exhilaration. On a practical level, you can use curiosity to help your kids develop their interests, create family fun, increase the likelihood that prospective clients will be interested in your services, make managers more effective, and help shape a company that is an exciting and enthusiastic place to work.

Consider the familiar expression, "Curiosity killed the cat, and satisfaction brought him back." Since cats have nine lives, there must have been at least nine situations in which the cat's curiosity *demanded satisfaction.* Thus, in homage to your evolutionary catlike heritage, let's look at nine scenarios where curiosity is life-enhancing.

"How can I get this person to be curious about a task so that she will *approach* it with enthusiasm?" is the question you'd ask yourself.

In each of the nine situations, observe that the key is leveraging the collative properties—novelty, complexity, information gaps, conflicting ideas—into play. The more skillful you are at using curiosity, the richer the rewards in your life. I'll show you how to strategically use your curiosity instinct in your master bedroom, your kid's playroom, at parties, and during sales presentations.

Mother Kink

"How can you enhance your sex life?" was the seminar question. On stage were three "sex experts." The first says to have open communication with your partner, expressing your desires. The second offers the advice to focus on enjoying other parts of your relationship, and your sex life gets better.

The third expert is Mother Nature. Her advice is the most interesting response, so naturally, seminar participants want to know more, perhaps because of the numerous studies that show many married individuals, after the age of 40, are dissatisfied with their sexual relationship. Many studies also indicate that approximately half the married population experiences a diagnosable sexual dysfunction, *inhibited sexual desire*, commonly described as not being turned on to your mate.

Apparently, many people would feel more satisfied with their life if their sexual relationship was enhanced, so they were interested to hear what Mother Nature meant when she answered: Stimulate sexual curiosity. I'll explain.

First, you are hardwired for sexual arousal, and this hardwiring serves the purpose of motivating you to explore your environment for a mate, a mission by the age of forty that is typically accomplished. Also, remember that the evolutionary function of sex is reproduction, to pass on your genes. Most likely, if you are over 40, this mission has been accomplished, too. To the point that these goals have been accomplished, a large portion of your sexual curiosity has been satisfied, which means you have less energy for sex.

Because sexual arousal requires energy, start to Alpha up arousal immediately. It is hard to be sexually aroused when you are tired, so the more energy you have in general, the sexier you can be.

Next, your sexual curiosity is aroused by the *novelty*, the newness of the stimuli. The new girl and guy in school get a lot of attention, since both are novel stimuli to the more familiar students who fill the school or office cafeteria. People on the block are always curious to see what the new neighbor looks like.

You might be deliriously in love with your partner, but with each sexual interaction, a degree of curiosity is satisfied, and sexual arousal is slightly diminished, too. To cut to the chase, every sexual interaction you have with your partner diminishes sexual curiosity because each sexual interaction increases sexual familiarity. Familiarity is the enemy of curiosity, and in the context of sex, it inhibits sexual arousal. Studies, for example, show repetitive sexual stimuli inevitably become less sexually arousing.

Here's one tip: Think again about going to your favorite restaurant to start off what you hope to be a romantic and sexy evening. Mother Nature would tell you to go to a new "hot" spot, one that you can both be aroused to go to, not one that keeps you in a comfort arousal zone. The *novelty* adds arousal in the form of excitement. This is what you need. In other words, you need some kink, a curve, something different, something novel.

The most crucial point: Novelty must not be so new that it creates avoidance or anxiety arousal. This is exactly the mistake that many couples make when they try to step up sexual arousal—they introduce *too much novelty*, and this stimulates anxiety/avoidance arousal, which instigates the opposite behavior of what you desire.

"Take your partner away for a romantic and hot weekend" is the best advice from love gurus. Many a partner can testify how he planned to do just that, only to find the evenings ended with arguments. Underlying this outcome is that the activity was too novel in its intent to stimulate sexual arousal, and thus created more sexual pressure than pleasure.

The specific advice to follow is you can sex up your relationship by using novelty to stimulate sexual arousal but, *you have to regulate the arousal created by novelty so that it is experienced as pleasurable rather than not*. Pleasurable arousal creates approach behavior.

Couples have different comfort and optimal sexual arousal levels, so what is highly sexually provocative to one is tame to another. But each couple has a respective sexual comfort arousal zone—one that, for the couple that wants some heat, needs to be increased and can be by *appropriate novelty*.

A subtle change in hair style might pique your partner, but wearing a wig, changing hair color, or an extreme haircut might do the opposite.

Changing the bed sheets to a different shade, dimming the lights, or adding music can arouse sexual attention, but going directly to velvet sheets and strobe lights might be too much—or might not.

Gradual increments in arousal are pleasurable, and extremes are not. This is also true for sexual arousal and is a point to remember. It is why many couples find massaging each other to be erotically stimulating and the same for extended foreplay.

Gradual sexual arousal is pleasurable and builds excitement because it stimulates sexual curiosity that seeks to be satisfied, thus instigating a heightened sexual response—the heat you desire.

Also note: *Sexual subtlety* is more arousing than sexual explicitness. This is so because subtlety is harder to interpret—a smile can be a friendly gesture from one person or an invitation for sex from another. Who is to know for sure? The subtleness creates an information gap, a sexual mystery that arouses our sexual curiosity. As long as the sexual subtlety isn't threatening, it will instigate approach behavior, a move so to speak.

For sure, many reasons cause a lack of sexual interest or a disturbance in our sexual interactions—far too many to discuss. Nevertheless, sometimes, more often than you think, you can sexy things up with some subtle novelty, some Mother Nature kink.

The Curious Presentation

A few weeks after a presentation I had given to a financial service company, an excited investment consultant called me to report how using curiosity helped him wow a bunch of "high asset" clients. "I gave a curious presentation," he proudly told me.

The details: Like many financial advisors, he was encouraged to give presentations to prospective clients for the obvious purpose of picking up some business. So, he had a room filled with approximately 30 "high net" clients—the "whales" who can make a huge difference in your income. Mind you, most of the individuals in the room had busy lives, and it is not uncommon for people to walk out of such presentations if their interest is not captured quickly.

When the prospective clients took their seats, he put curiosity into play by passing out to each individual a colorfully wrapped box. "Just hold it, but you can shake it, if you like."

When everyone had one, he told them, "What's inside your boxes could change your life, your family's life, and your friends' lives."

"What do you think is in your box?" he asked, but no one responded.

"I will give you a clue. It has something to do with finance."

Now, there were some responses: "A list of stock tips." "Some inside information." "Swiss bank account key."

Before he told them to open it, he responded to their guesses. First, he told them that he does give stock tips, and from there he went on to explain his financial management/advisor philosophy. He took advantage of the "inside information" response by giving his passionate rant on ethics and integrity and made it clear to everyone that his professional conduct was straight-arrow. To the gentleman who guessed a Swiss bank account, he explained his financial strategies in global markets, and the current returns on such investments.

He then thanked them for coming and looked forward to their using the box's contents to enhance their lives. Like children, they all pulled off the shiny bow, tore the wrapping paper, and opened the box; there they saw what could change their lives—a nice business card case with his card inside. He told me that a half dozen individuals phoned him during the next few days, a good return on his investment.

Do you see how curiosity was stimulated? First is the *novelty* of the presentation, exemplified by giving each a curious object rather than the standard folder of papers. The object, wrapped with green and gold paper and tied with a silver bow, took advantage of stimulus properties, such as attractiveness.

Note how the advisor immediately created an *information gap* by asking them to guess the contents, creating uncertainty and stimulating more *curiosity arousal* restless to be satisfied. By asking/*questioning* them to guess, he increased their *arousal level*, and he also gave them time to *explore* the situation. By giving a clue—"Something to do with finance"—he focused their interest and kept the *complexity* of the situation at the appropriate level so that they would continue to be curious. By not letting them open the curious object with its *surprise contents* until the very end, he kept their arousal and their interest high, made it fun, and evidently, got several clients to be curious about him and want to learn how he can be of service.

The bottom line when it comes to presentations: PowerPoint out—curiosity in!

Young at Heart

Senile depression afflicts millions of people, but sitting around the house, making their lives small and familiar, serves to exacerbate it. Accordingly, baby boomers are smart to encourage their parents to get out and about, do new activities, keep sharp, and keep developing their interests. Keeping your parents' curiosity instincts alive and well will help them feel young, energized, and explorative. With these factors in play, they can approach more potential life-enhancing activities so that their last fairy tales can come true.

There's a problem, though. As your parents get older, the curiosity instinct diminishes, partly because there is less need for sexual and intellectual curiosity. Sexual activity decreases, and so does a thirst for knowledge. So, right off the bat, there is less curiosity arousal to work with and less motivation to instigate exploring and investigating behavior.

Another problem makes it even more difficult to stimulate your parents' curiosity instincts, especially those in their mid-seventies. Their aversion to loss is probably at its highest, so it is extremely important for them to feel safe and secure. Staying home in front of the TV is safe and secure, but it's the opposite of curious behavior.

When you mix lower general curiosity level with highest loss aversion, you can see why so many baby boomers are frustrated that their parents stick close to home, when they could be doing many life-enhancing activities.

What the children try usually backfires. Their suggestions are too dramatic—an unpleasant shift in physical arousal, which causes avoidant behavior. "I don't want to. I'm not interested," is how it plays out.

As we have been discussing, you should enhance your parents' lives by reviving their curiosity instincts, the ones they used all the time when they were the age of their grandchildren. But do it slowly and gradually. To do this most effectively, think of an activity, such as joining a club, enrolling in a class, or taking a trip, that you believe they would enjoy or always wanted to do, something that would currently enrich their days.

Instead of urging or even encouraging, follow the strategy of increasing their curiosity arousal by providing little pieces of pleasurable information so that they want to hear more. Inevitably, you are going to get your parents to be so curious that they are motivated and energized for action.

For example, instead of urging your parents or widowed parent to take a trip or enroll in a class, make them curious by every so often making comments about the trip you know they've always wanted to take. "Hey, my friends just got back from Japan. They had a great time." A few weeks later, "I saw a great travel show on Tokyo. Fantastic places to see there." Weeks later, "You know, my friend told me they saw a lot of seniors traveling in groups when they were in Japan." These are all gradual setups for: "I'm having lunch with a client who's a travel agent. Want me to ask her for brochures on senior tours?"

In other words, be strategic: Stimulate gradual curiosity by incrementally filling *information gaps* with *pleasurable* pieces of information. This inspires *approach behavior with enthusiasm.*

Stimulating your parents' curiosity instinct is not an overnight process—it can take a few months. But if you take the time to do it, you will keep them young at heart and thus increase the chance that some of their fairy tales will come true.

Curious Family Fun

All families and couples like to have fun together. Fun makes people feel good, more productive, healthier, and happier. Fun generates positive feelings and emotions, so it is easy to see how natural selection would favor fun-loving families and couples. The positive emotions are contagious and increase bonding and cohesiveness. I'd be hard-pressed to recall a couple or a family who came to therapy with the complaint, "We're having too much fun."

Couples and families can have fun in many ways, but one of the ways you can have *much more of it* is if you remember a hardwiring point from Mother Nature: "It is fun to be curious," so the plan here is to *use curiosity to stimulate fun.* A curious *surprise* will help.

Surprise is activated by a sharp increase in neural stimulation. The external condition for surprise is any sudden and unexpected event. The event may be a clap of thunder, the crackle of fireworks, or people jumping out of the closet yelling: "Surprise!"

From an evolutionary standpoint, its primary function is to help prepare the individual to deal effectively with the new or sudden event. Natural selection favors those who can deal with sudden change. Failure, for example, to react rapidly at the sudden appearance of a predatory animal or threatening situation could result in serious harm or death.

A few brief points about surprise will enlighten about how you can use it to create curious fun.

First, like most people, I'm sure you've felt surprised, but it is probably a feeling that is difficult to describe. One reason is the *feeling* lasts only momentarily. A second reason is that there is little *conscious* thought. Both of these points need to be manipulated for curious fun.

Next, studies show that surprise is characterized by a high degree of *pleasantness arousal*; when people are asked to recall a time when they were surprised, they overwhelmingly recall a situation that turned out to be happy and pleasant. In these moments, they experienced *pleasant physical arousal*.

This last point is the basis for using surprise to create curious fun. At the moment of surprise, you do not know exactly how to react. There is a feeling of *uncertainty* created by the sudden unexpected event. It is this uncertainty that makes surprise a *collative property*—its unfamiliarity as it fits into what an individual knows—that can stimulate curiosity and create fun arousal.

You can manipulate the briefness, its positive nature, and the uncertainty to intensify a surprise. First, surprise is experienced as being pleasurable, *so increase the frequency of surprise* in your marriage and family environments. And, *make surprise arousal last longer by increasing the length of the surprise moment.* Increasing the length of the surprise moment allows the individual to enjoy the pleasurable feelings longer.

Now, you leverage the fact that there is little conscious thought during a surprise moment by doing the exact opposite of conventional surprise: Openly state *a pleasant surprise is in the air*. In other words, *don't spring a surprise* on your partner or your kids. Instead, for example, ask them to guess what the surprise is and give them all sorts of positive hints.

"See if you can guess where we are going to dinner," creates much more fun than, "I made a reservation at The Ivy." "I bet you will never guess what I got you for your birthday." Creating the suspense two weeks before an event turns one day of fun into fourteen.

Note how information gaps play with ambiguity—by asking a question, you create an information gap that stimulates curiosity—a need to know starts the fun: "Make three guesses." "One more clue, Dad!" "What do I get if I guess right?" Are all phrases of playful curiosity.

One couple I know used curious fun every year when they had to attend a friend's dreaded annual Halloween party. "It was always a pain deciding what we should go as, and many times, we would argue. By the beginning of October, we would be stressed out over a Halloween party," they would say.

They turned it around by, instead of deciding their costumes together, they decided to surprise each other. Three weeks before the party, each had great fun wondering what the other had chosen, and each had fun stimulating the curiosity of the other by giving hints and clues. And, the anticipation of seeing each other ready to go to the party added enthusiasm. "It's so much more fun now that we surprise each other," they say.

For family practice, make it the responsibility for each member of your clan to tell another that in the next few weeks, he or she is in for a pleasant surprise. To increase their enjoyment, give each other three clues before the surprise moment. In fact, you can add to the playful suspense by making the clues appropriately complex—not too hard, not too easy.

If your family resists playing the surprise game, stimulate the family identity until every member yells, "Surprise!"

Curious Conversation

Whether you are trying to meet someone on J-date or pick up a customer, there will be no action if you can't generate some curiosity. Getting noticed is your start, so you might find implementing the curious conversation to be helpful.

Natural selection would be much kinder to those who practiced curious conversation; these would be your ancestors who could develop relationships more effectively and be better negotiators in their "business dealings," since they could *arouse* others to pay a higher price.

I profess that the curious conversation is an advanced technique for stimulating curiosity, too advanced for some to even attempt. It takes time to practice and is difficult to master, but for those who do, it is enhancing to you because it gives you more of a chance to inter- est people who *you want interested in you,* and this gives you the opportunity to enhance your life, be it at work or in a social scene.

The action prelude starts by realizing the goal of the curious conversation: Get people to want to hear more about you—or your product. In curiosity lingo, your effort will be directed to making it pleasantly arousing for the person to approach you. You do this, of course, by implanting a conversation that makes them curious about you.

Sometimes the time to implement is a given time, such as when you are meeting a person for the first time, either formally or casually at a party. Other times, in the midst of an encounter, you have an opportunity to implement curious conversation. At either time, though, the goal is the same: to get the person to want to know more about you.

You accomplish this goal by blending and using information gaps, novelty, surprise, and pleasant arousal into your conversations. It is complicated, but less so if you break it down.

In contrast to conventional, conversational advice, you don't pique interest by being up-front and personal immediately. Slow down "the getting to know you" process by creating information gaps.

Example: You are at a party (trade show, conference, convention, hotel) and see a cool cat (customer, potential client, potential contact) who spikes your curiosity. But now you have to get them to be curious about you. Moments into the conversation, you intentionally work in "I graduated from college in the '80s" and this creates an information gap. "What college?" is the question that will most likely be asked to fill in the gap. At this point, most people respond with the college name, which might end the conversation—curiosity satisfied—and with it, you have sent that cool cat to prowl elsewhere.

It could be different. Curious conversation dictates that the next response would be ambiguous, perhaps a reference to geography: "In New England." The intent of such a response is to make the cat more curious. "Where in New England?" Again, create an information gap: "Boston," and so on, until you fill in the final blank.

The point, though, is that by using curious conversation, you have extended a momentary encounter into a longer moment, and that few extra moments gives you more time to engage the person; a chance is created to turn the person's initial interest excitement in you to a depth of interest—a desire to know more about you.

A financial advisor used the same process curing a social event. "What do you do?" was the stimulant. His response was, "Protect people." This led to a lengthy encounter, whereas "I'm a financial advisor for Ron Securities" might send the person running.

Novelty comes into talk, too. Interesting ways of expressing your thoughts spark attention of others; "I've never heard that before" is a response from your conversational partner that will take you further than "I've heard that before."

Curiosity words help too—"might," "may," "perhaps," "could," and "maybe"—all typically facilitate conversational length because they create ambiguity, and this instigates further conversation for clarification. Again, this provides more time to exchange ideas and allow others to become interested in you.

Sometimes, the curious conversation can be of minimal dialogue, yet take several hours. For instance, once when I was flying from New York to Los Angeles I sat next to the president of an upscale food chain in Los Angeles. I knew it well—excellent fruit.

Shortly into the flight, our conversation started and, upon learning of my trade, he became a class participant. He told me that his employees were taking advantage of the food discount he offered them. Three days before a specific date, employees were allowed to buy a healthy amount of fresh foods they wanted at a significant discount. The problem was they were exercising that right before the prescribed date, and this was costing his chain money since there was less for full-paying customers, who were forced to look elsewhere. He told me that he was very good to his employees, giving bonuses, company cars to his regional managers, and food discounts. He felt betrayed and told me that he was now going to tell them that the food discount was over. "Full price or shop elsewhere would be his new motto," he told me.

His behavior—head turning to me—told me he wanted my response, but I also had enough similar experiences to know that a quick response often ends the conversation. "Well, that's one way to handle it," is all I said. But it created an information gap.

I did have the urge to give a mini-lecture, but part of being masterful in curious conversation is regulating your own arousal during the moments of curiosity arousal. At the time, I regulated my arousal by turning my attention to making some work-related notes.

Regulating your arousal and keeping yourself mum allows you to provide the person time to think about what you said, to raise possibilities, to become curious until satisfaction is needed. Several hours later, as the meal was being served, he said, "Okay, so what is another way I can handle this."

"Later," I told him, "after I eat and watch the movie."

You can learn how to use your curiosity instincts to develop your children's interest and even deal with intrusive people, by reading the next chapter.

22

Curiosity Satisfied

If you're still feeling cat-like, I'll satisfy your curiosity by illustrating how the genius of your instincts can be used in your kid's room, the boardroom, with self-development, and with nosey people.

Raising Interest Rates

"IIe's not interested in anything." "She has no idea what she is interested in." "You still don't know what you're interested in?" These are phrases that begin a common parental litany that strongly suggests that, unlike Wall Street players, parents always would like to raise the interest rates of their most important bonds—their children. It is a smart investment strategy when you consider the life-long returns.

Interest is the most frequently experienced positive emotion. It provides much of the motivation for being creative and for learning the skills and competencies every child needs to master. These dividends are inarguably life-enhancing.

You might recall from an earlier example, that following the *interest behaviors* of another could alert you to a potential danger, such as a predator approaching. This is called *interest excitement*, and you can clearly see its evolutionary value.

There is also *depth interest*, and the feelings that accompany it, too, are pleasurable. The feelings serve the purpose of keeping the individual positively focused for a much longer period.

Interest—curiosity—leads to artistic, scientific, and social pursuits that result in achievements that secure individual niches and advance civilization, too.

Since curiosity is the instinct that initiates the development of interests, Mother Nature would tell you that if you want your kids to be "interest bullish," stimulate their curiosity with the following two thoughts in mind: *yourself* and *imagination*.

As a parent, you are much more likely to nourish strong interests in your children if you are open to change and novelty than if you are rigid and prefer to live by established dogmas. By your actions and words, you can either encourage or discourage the curiosity that sparks the interests and exploratory behavior of your children. Curious and open parents transmit this and "model" it to their children. Thus, if you have started to stimulate your own curiosity instincts, you are already helping your children, and if you are not, you have some insight into why your kids "have no interests."

Most of your efforts to raise your children's interest rates occur in their early to teen years, but without a doubt, you can still help raise their interest in later years.

Mother Nature can tell you a few basic *interest builders*: Encourage questions, engage in plenty of fun activities, allow your children to make choices, and allow your children to try many activities. These are interest builders because they are *curiosity-friendly*—they instigate exploratory behavior with a *pleasurable sense of arousal*. But don't force an interest or pressure them. Pressure creates *avoidance arousal*, and the activity takes on negative feelings.

Most importantly, emphasize your child's freedom to play, to enjoy make-believe and fantasy and to allow and encourage her to move freely from the real to the imaginary world. It has a strong and lasting influence on your child's future ability to experience potential interest arousal because it introduces the conception of *possibility*.

The world of possibility is always ambiguous and, therefore, is a giant playground for you to help your child—at any age. Initiate, pursue, and develop interests that might turn into the reality of achievement. In the world of possibility, your children can be interested in whatever they want. Novelty can run rampant, since different interests can be imagined continually.

Furthermore, the world of possibility allows children the chance to play out *their interest stories* with a glimpse into a possible ending that may either stimulate the interest toward reality, or dismiss it, on the grounds that it is no longer interesting (pleasantly arousing). "What if I became a forest ranger? What would I do? Would I like it? Where would I live?"

What this means for you, the parent, is that you can stimulate your child's interest via *imagination*, a process that Mother Nature has hardwired into humans. Imagination allows you to conjecture up scenarios in the absence of real stimuli.

Imagination is an evolved adaptation for survival: Imagining how you would defend yourself against a charging predator (destructive criticism from your boss) would come in handy if the situation arose in reality, since natural selection would favor the prepared mind. Furthermore, those ancestors whose imagination excelled had the edge of being able to create and innovate, processes that are life-enhancing.

A couple of ways to mix curiosity and imagination for interest development is to ask questions whose answers require your child to use imagination. Work into conversations *curiosity statements* designed to get your kids to think about developing a new interest or trying a new activity.

Pay attention to question structure. "*What* are you interested in?" is more on the interrogation side and elicits discomfort arousal because it demands a specific response. In contrast, the parent who asks, "What *could* you be interested in?" arouses curiosity because the word "could" stimulates the teen to *consider*, and the stimulated thoughts might result in exploratory behavior. "Wonder" and "might" are also words that can stimulate "curious thinking."

When a child is young, his curiosity is captured by novel objects, bright colors, and moving objects. Take advantage of stimulus properties to stimulate and create interest. Parents giving their child a bath in a bathtub filled with a little moving fishing toy and a bunch of colorful spongy fish might be the parents whose kid several years later says, "Let's go fishing together."

The parent on a summer evening walk with her seven-year-old, points up and says, "Imagine yourself going to the moon," might be stimulating his daughter's interest in science, astronomy, or physics.

A parent playing with her five-year-old son and his stuffed animals might say, "Oh, Horsey looks sick. Make believe you are the doctor and take care of him." That might just be creating an interest that leads to veterinarian school.

Years later, the same father or mother might help his or her child clarify an interest in a veterinarian specialty by asking, "Can you imagine yourself working in a laboratory and wearing a white coat? Will you enjoy that type of work ten years from now? Are you going to be happy dealing with just this one type of problem?" These questions take advantage of the same imaginary play, the difference being the son is now older to assess the reality of his interest level and whether to continue developing it. Tip: The more details imagined, the easier it is to assess a true level of interest.

A first-year college student who says, "I don't know what I am interested in," is not helped with, "You will figure it out," or "You have plenty of time," or "What do you like?" A better response, one that helps him be curious and could stimulate him, would be to sit down and stimulate his imagination: "Well, what type of environment can you imagine yourself in? Can you imagine yourself working on your own? Imagine if you become a doctor or nurse—the long hours, dealing with sick people—can you imagine yourself doing that?"

Remember that interest is a pleasant emotion, so the act of using your hardwired imagination to conjecture up interests and their stories becomes a pleasurable activity and inevitably becomes self-generating. You experience this process when you imagine yourself doing a different job—your imagination allows you to play out the results of your interest. It can motivate you to make a change or motivate a quick return to your current interest.

Getting your children to imagine the world of interests in the safety of imagination increases the chances that their interest rates will increase.

Curious Criticism

Not long ago, I gave the top 100 partners of one of the world's largest service consulting firms a curiosity assignment. They were to schedule a meeting with one of their top clients for the sole purpose of soliciting criticism.

Criticism—giving and taking it—had been the topic of the seminar, so the rationale was clear, and they had gotten a lot of new information about taking criticism positively. They knew that one of the best ways to accelerate your own learning and development is to be curious about yourself; to discover, explore, and investigate yourself so that you can determine what has an impact and gets results in your life and how to discern the areas in your life that you need to develop.

Self-aware people have a critical edge, and this is as true today as it was hundreds of thousands of years ago. Early man who used his curiosity to find out how he could be more effective and what he might be doing to impede his own success was an ancestor who was creating "self-help genes."

"What's the best way to learn about yourself?" was the first question, the class opener. "Take some psychological testing," was one response. "Go to a therapist," was another. Somebody earnestly offered, "Reflect and take stock of yourself."

"Here's another. Ask for criticism." My suggestion surprised the group, and they became more attentive.

I explained that criticism is all around us—in our work relationships, marriage, parenting, and friends. It is everywhere. Received openly, it enhances all aspects of our lives, including making a performance appraisal more useful, making a marriage more satisfying, and developing our leadership capacities. Literally dozens of studies support that giving and taking criticism well is crucial to our success in life.

Yet, most of us, including those given the assignment, find hearing criticism about ourselves and/or our work to be upsetting. In our minds, we think of criticism as a hostile attack. In our bodies, we feel it with a fear and anxiety response—avoidance arousal. Today, that translates into defensive behavior, which, more often than not, decelerates our learning and often prevents us from profiting from the feedback.

"Be curious about criticism," is the prescription for regulating your defensive arousal. This allows you to approach criticism with a friendlier attitude.

To spark your curiosity and buffer your defensiveness, develop a *curious attitude* about criticism: "Criticism is information that can help me grow. How can this information help me? What is it the person wants me to know?"

Accelerate your learning by soliciting criticism from those around you. And, phrase it positively. "What are some things that I could be doing better?" Not: "What am I doing wrong?"

When you hear the responses, delay your own, which most likely, even with your new curious attitude, will be defensive. Instead, thank them for their thoughts and spend the next few days not retreating from, but instead exploring the implications and applications of what they told you. Equally important, how do you *feel* when you learn about yourself?

It won't take long for you to realize that you will not die from what you heard—criticism is not a lion, tiger, or bear, "Oh, my!" Evaluate the criticisms with curiosity, the attitude that will most help you discover the perceptions of others so that you can profit from them.

What Is the Curious Corporate Culture?

I'll satisfy your curiosity quickly. The curious corporate culture is exactly what you imagine it would be: a successful one with a strong ecological niche. This is the payoff for a culture that initiates, develops, and rewards exploratory and investigative behavior. By definition, all the cutting-edge organizations—private and public, medical, educational, or consumer electronics—have a curious culture. Curiosity accelerates learning and gives them the breakthrough edge.

I've been lucky to work with several curious cultures, so I can zip you through a few of their rituals that continually apply *collative* stimuli to maximize and reward innovation.

At all levels, people's curiosities are stimulated by the assignment of *interesting problems* whose answers help enhance some aspect of organizational effectiveness. *Interesting* captures attention, and *problem assignments* create information gaps. One implementation would be to have a once a month *curious problem staff meeting*, where the staff is given a problem to solve and encouraged to work it out with each other. The answer, sometimes, will be far from perfect, but the exploratory behavior the task stimulates inevitably pays off later.

Whereas most performance reviews focus on goal achievement, the emphasis on individual development and interests is crucial to a curious culture performance appraisal. A curiosity stimulating performance appraisal questions: "What type of project interests you the most?" "What type of training can help you meet your interests?" The more a work assignment can be personalized, the more there is enthusiasm and motivation to work hard and be creative. Here's an untapped management development technique and recommendation: Stimulate curiosity and develop interest to improve performance.

Regulating organizational anxiety is crucial, too. Don't institute huge, sudden changes. Recall that anxiety is uncertainty, and when uncertainty is too high (too novel), the avoidance response kicks in. You retreat. Maintaining a questioning environment, encouraging people to contribute their interests, and keeping open, accurate, and frequent communication are all ways to regulate organizational arousal and keep its curious soul alive.

Switching up the physical environment and encouraging people to know each other, too, can keep it interesting at work. How often does your company cafeteria menu change? Curious corporate cultures thrive on novelty—it is an attention grabber, be it a new food offering in the cafeteria or new artwork in the hallways every month. How about using "novel lunch" day, a fun event in which, once a month, employees are asked to join a table and meet new people. "Be curious about your coworker" is a possible program slogan, and it is fun since it is fun to be curious. Novelty stimulates excitement. It keeps people juiced up. New types of assignments mixed with gradual increments of difficulty are a natural for keeping people motivated and committed.

Don't forget surprise. I once worked with a company whose president thrived on having surprise theme parties for corporate morale. Only his insiders would know. A few clues were given out (just like Nature prescribes), and everybody would be excited to enter the party room. Surprise, as implemented here, became a tool to generate long durations of pleasant arousal at work.

Curiosity Shut Up!

It is one thing to use curiosity to stimulate learning, creativity, and other forms of enhancement, but it is quite another when curiosity invades your privacy, whether it is at work, home, or in the neighborhood. Here, *you* are the curious object of another—a parent, partner, child, coworker, boss, assistant, client, friend, family member, or next-door neighbor. The person's curiosity is directed at you in the form of continually asking you intrusive questions, wanting to know all the details of your life, even about those matters that you want to keep private. The end result: The curiosity about you is driving you crazy and making the relationship stressful. This is when you need to *shut up curiosity*.

People, like animals, are hardwired with sense of personal boundary to provide an area of safety and security. Our boundaries are flexible; we adapt them to the situation. When your defined boundary is intruded, you feel distressed. Your "space" is being invaded, and with it your sense of security and safety.

In the case of animals, such as wolves and dogs, the boundary space is defined in physical distance. In humans, boundary is defined in psychological space. Intrusive people make you *feel uncomfortable*. How do you push them back without having to get hostile?

Conventional wisdom recommends: "It's none of your business." "How is that your concern?" "That's a pretty personal question, isn't it?" Instead, remember that it is natural for people to be curious about you. Those ancestors who showed interest in others would be the first to realize the true motives of others, friend or foe—information for survival. Also, back on the Savannah, with people working closely together and living closely together, it became natural that they would become curious about each other and talk about each other, and this served the purpose of developing communication in the community. Use this evolutionary insight to take *advantage* of the curiosity that is offending you.

There are many ways to explain the motivation and dynamics of an intrusive person, but for sure, the person's curiosity about you takes him out of his arousal comfort zone, and this initiates intrusive exploratory and investigative behavior via incessant questions that probe into your life. The intrusive behavior is how the intruder closes information gaps and returns to his own comfort zone. Thus, every time you relent and answer questions, you are satisfying the intruder's curiosity. Instead of "shutting them up," it backfires on you. The person asks you even more personal questions.

If you don't want the person's curiosity to kill you, generate a novel response, one that will *oversatisfy the person's curiosity*. In essence, when you *oversatisfy curiosity*, you provide so many details that you bore them to death, similar to when you are curious to hear a lecture until, after an hour of it, you have heard enough. Too much information: That's your goal to get the intruder to say "enough." In clinical parlance, this would be referred to as *creating change through paradox*. The "Case of the Curious Mom," illustrates the strategy to perfection.

For years, Mom was intensely curious about every aspect of her only daughter's life. She engaged in frequent interrogations about her daughter's school day, social life, even her personal fantasy life. At times, the curiosity—to the interrogation level—would become intense, and the daughter would erupt into tears and anger. But it only increased Mom's curiosity. Now she had to know why the tears and anger. This continued through junior high.

The first day of high school, the daughter turned the tables on her mother. Her father picked her up from school and warned her that Mom was waiting at home, curious about her daughter's first day. The anticipation of dealing with Curious Mom immediately made the daughter anxious, but before she could voice her complaints of Curious Mom, Dad offered a novel solution.

"Listen, you know your mother is going to interrogate you, so beat her to it. Before she can ask her first question, say you want to tell her everything about your day—from 7:45 a.m. to 3:00 p.m. Tell her to sit down with you and tell her everything, the more detailed and boring the better." The daughter followed his instructions and spent a full 40 minutes telling Curious Mom every detail of every class, including what was on the cafeteria menu and everything she could remember from science and math class.

The next day, the father again picked up his daughter and instructed her to follow the same plan. "The key, "he reminded her, "is to tell her in excruciating detail." The daughter obeyed and spent the time sitting with her mother, telling her all.

The third day, the procedure was repeated, but this time, as soon as the daughter asked her mother to sit so she could tell her the events of the day, Curious Mom, a bit perturbed, said, "Hey, I don't need to hear every detail of your life. Keep it to yourself!"

What accounts for the mother's response is that the daughter decreased the mother's curiosity arousal by giving her *too much infor-mation*: "Enough already." The daughter's approach behavior, telling the mother *more* than she wanted to know, created avoidance behav-ior in the Curious Mom because "boring" arousal is something we look to escape. Thus, Curious Mom wanted to hear less, not more. At a party, you often want to escape the person who is giving you details of her life—it bores you, so you escape. Similarly, increasing the information you give your micromanaging boss is an effective way to get him to back off.

If you have a curious intruder in your life, you might want to try this strategy. In the case of the Curious Mom, Mother Nature would clearly say that it is one of the few times when you can tell a mom to shut up—but do it nicely.

Conclusion

Use Your Natural Genius

The primary message of this book has been that you are hard-wired to be successful, that you have in your possession a powerful set of instinctual tools that enhance your life and can help you solve some of life's most daunting problems.

Indeed, their effectiveness in helping you has literally stood the test of time. They guided your ancestors, and they will guide your great-great-grandchildren.

Your instincts, then, are far from the common perception of being dark and uncivilized. Quite the contrary; they are the ultimate life-enhancers. Reconnect with them, listen to them, let their natural genius guide you to a more authentic and vibrant life.

Appendix

The Life Enhancement
Instinct Inventory

The "Life Enhancement Instinct Inventory" is designed to assist you in enhancing your adaptive capacities to the challenges and problems you encounter in your daily environments.

An overview of the procedure is to first familiarize yourself with the function of each instinctual adaptive tool, as well as examples of behaviors that suggest you are either practicing or not practicing the respective tool. After thoughtful reflection, assess yourself on how well you practice each instinctual adaptive process in the context of your everyday working environment.

From this data, you select specific instinctual tools to use more effectively and devise a plan as to how you will implement your use.

Finally, you assess your progress and repeat the process—continually, so that you are using your links to success.

Step I: Know Your Tools

Use the following chart to familiarize yourself with the six instinctual tools and their purpose.

Instinctual Tool	Purpose
Shelter seeking	To select an empowering environment
Care soliciting	To protect your vulnerabilities
Care giving	To develop others
Co-op	To stimulate cooperation
Beautify	To pull people toward you
Curiosity	To accelerate your learning

Step II: Assessing Instinctual Connection

The following six questions and five behaviors/feelings under each are designed to help you assess how well you are applying your instincts of success. After thoughtful reflection on each item, self-evaluate on a scale from 1 to 9; a score of 9 indicates that (based on the purpose of the behavior and the samples listed) you are applying the specific instinct of success.

1. Shelter seeking behavior: Do you put yourself in empowering environments?
   a. Surround myself with supportive people.
   b. Feel good at work.
   c. Am in the right job.
   d. Company/organization helps me grow.
   e. Feel secure in my work environment.

   Evaluation: 1—-2—-3—-4—-5—-6—-7—-8—-9

2. Care soliciting: Do you protect your vulnerabilities?
 a. Take criticism productively
 b. Comfortable asking for help
 c. Like to learn from others
 d. Show my feelings
 e. Actively support people who help you
     Evaluation: 1—-2—-3—-4—-5—-6—-7—-8—-9

3. Care giving behavior: Do you develop others?
 a. Like coaching people
 b. Help others deal with personal problems
 c. Improve performance of others
 d. Often help assistants
 e. Give positive criticism
     Evaluation: 1—-2—-3—-4—-5—-6—-7—-8—-9

4. Co-op behavior: Do you stimulate cooperation?
 a. Like to cooperate more than compete
 b. Experience little conflict with others
 c. Aware of team goals
 d. Involve others in decision making
 e. Frequently help coworkers
     Evaluation: 1—-2—-3—-4—-5—-6—-7—-8

5. Beautify: Do you pull people toward you?
 a. People want to be with me.
 b. Have a good sense of humor.
 c. Often encourage others.
 d. Coworkers ask for my input.
 e. Others support me.
     Evaluation: 1—-2—-3—-4—-5—-6—-7—-8—-9

6. Curious behavior: Do you accelerate your learning?

    a. Actively learn new things

    b. Like to do new activities

    c. Comfortable with uncertainty

    d. Seek out challenges

    e. Are you an active person?

       Evaluation: 1—-2—-3—-4—-5—-6—-7—-8—-9

Step III: Review Your Evaluations

Starting with your lowest evaluation (for equal evaluations, begin with your preference), identify ways in which you can apply the specific instinctual behavior and expected outcomes based on the purpose of your action. Record your responses in the following format.

Instinctual Tool	Instinctual Connection	Expected Outcome
Care Giving	Positive criticism	Improved performance in others; positive self-feelings

Step IV: Monitor Your Progress

When you begin to experience the expected outcomes, move on to the next lowest evaluated instinctual behavior and repeat the process. Keep doing this until you can give yourself a 9 in applying each of the instinctual tools. You will then be using the genius of your instincts.

References

The following are primary references for this book, each providing valuable examples, specific empirical studies, and greater understanding of evolutionary instinctual concepts.

Archer, J. *Exploration in Animals and Humans*. UK: Van Nostrand Reinhold, 1983.

Baron, Robert. *Mastering Social Psychology*, tenth edition. New York: Allyn & Bacon, 2006.

Berlyne, D. *Conflict, Arousal, and Curiosity*. New York: McGraw Hill, 1960.

——. "A Theory of Human Curiosity." *British Journal of Psychology* 45: 180-91.

Binmore, K. *Game Theory and the Social Contract, vol. 1: Playing Fair*. Cambridge, MA: MIT Press, 1994.

Buss, David. *Evolutionary Psychology: The New Science of the Mind*. New York: Allyn & Bacon, 2003.

Cosmides, L., and J. Tooby. *Evolutionary Psychology: A Primer*. Santa Barbara, CA: Center for Evolutionary Psychology, University of California, Santa Barbara, 2004.

Darwin, C. R. *The Expression of Emotions in Man and Animals*. London: John Murray, 1872.

Dawkins, S. *The Selfish Gene*. Oxford University Press, 1976.

Edelman, Susan. *Curiosity and Exploration*. Northridge, CA: California State University, 1997.

Epps, Stephanie. *The Social Behavior of Beef Cattle*. Department of Animal Sciences, Texas A&M University, 2002.

Hardy, S. *Mother Nature: Maternal Instincts and How They Shape the Human Species*. New York: Ballantine, 1999.

Hatfield, Elaine. *Emotional Contagion*. Cambridge University Press, 1994.

Hebb, D. "Drives and the C.N.S. (Conceptual Nervous System)." *Psychological Review* 62: 243-45.

Heinsohn, R., and C. Packer. "Complex Cooperative Strategies in Group-Territorial African Lions." *Science* 269 (1995): 1260-62.

Izard, C. *The Face of Emotions*. New York: Appleton-Century-Crofts, 1971.

James, W. *Principles of Psychology*. New York: Holt, 1950 (1890 original publication).

Lorenz, K. *King Solomon's Rings*. London: Methuen, 1961.

McCullough, M. *Beyond Revenge: The Evolution of the Forgiveness Instinct*. New York: John Wiley & Sons, 2008.

Miller, Alan, and Kanazawa Sataoshi. *Why Beautiful People Have More Daughters*. New York: Penguin, 2007.

Nicholson, N. *Executive Instinct*. New York: Random House, 2001.

Novicel, Harvey. "The Role of Curiosity in Global Managers Decision-Making." *Journal of Leadership and Organizational Studies*, spring 2007.

O'Neal, Harold, and M. Drilling, eds. *Motivation: Theory and Research*. Hillsdale, NJ: Lawrence Erlbaum Associates, 1994.

Parker, C. "Reciprocal Altruism in Olive Baboons." *Nature* 265 (1977): 441-43.

Piner, S. *The Language Instincts*. London: Allen Lane, 1994.

Plutchick, R. *The Emotions: Facts, Theories, and a New Model*. New York: Random House, 1962.

Podell, R. *Contagious Emotions*. New York: Simon & Schuster, 1993.

Rapport, A. and A. M. Chummah. *Prisoner's Dilemma*. Ann Arbor: University of Michigan Press, 1965.

Ridley, Matt. *The Origins of Virtue*. Great Britain: Penguin Books, 1966.

Rodriguez, J. *History of the Dog*. Connecticut: Elite Canine, 2004.

Schmidt, Anthony. *New Aspects of Human Ethnology: Proceedings of the 13th Conference*. 1997.

Taylor, S. *The Tending Instinct*. New York: Times Books, 2002.

Tomkins, S. "Affect, Imagery, Consciousness" in vol. 1, *The Positive Affects*. New York: Springer, 1962.

——. "Affect, Imagery, Consciousness" in vol. 2, *The Negative Affects*. New York: Springer, 1962.

Trivers, R. L. "The Evolution of Reciprocal Altruism." *Quarterly Review of Biology* 46 (1971): 35-37.

Walker, Matt. *Fish That Fake Orgasms*. New York: St. Martin's Press, 2006.

Weisinger, H. *The Power of Positive Criticism*. New York: AMACOM, 2000.

Wilkinson, G. S. "Reciprocal Food Sharing in the Vampire Bat." *Nature* 308 (1984): 181-84.

INDEX

FINANCIAL TIMES

In an increasingly competitive world, it is quality
of thinking that gives an edge—an idea that opens new
doors, a technique that solves a problem, or an insight
that simply helps make sense of it all.

We work with leading authors in the various arenas
of business and finance to bring cutting-edge thinking
and best-learning practices to a global market.

It is our goal to create world-class print publications
and electronic products that give readers
knowledge and understanding that can then be
applied, whether studying or at work.

To find out more about our business
products, you can visit us at www.ftpress.com.